Handwriting Review

1995

Contents

ISBN 1 872832 05 9

The Handwriting Interest Group and its journal, *Handwriting Review,* aim to promote information and debate on the subject of handwriting. The views expresses in this journal are those of the writers and advertisers. They may be held by various members of the Group, but are not endorsed by the Handwriting Interest Group itself.

Printed by Bemrose-Shafron Printers (Ltd.),
       21, Chaser Court,
       Greyhound Park,
       Chester, CH1 4QQ

Editorial

The *Handwriting Review* is a journal which, it is hoped, will be of interest to all professionals interested in handwriting. Because it is produced in the United Kingdom, inevitably many of the papers make reference to the British Education system. However, papers are published from across the world. Issues in handwriting do not apply to any one system of writing or one educational sytem.

The *Handwriting Review 1995* is published at a time when we are promised a period of calm in the world of the National Curriculum, if not in the world of education in general. There is to be a five year moratorium on change. Teachers and other professionals with a major interest in the teaching of handwriting may perhaps have been a little dismayed that Handwriting as a separate Attainment Target has disappeared. Handwriting is now incorporated under the heading of Writing. However, the English document continues to make it clear that Handwriting is a skill which must be taught. As such it is listed under the Key Skills. The requirement to teach this important skill is also not just one for the Primary school, Paragraph 2.4 for Key Stages 3 and 4 states *"Pupils should be taught neat and legible **handwriting.** "* This is good news. There are children who still need to have help with their handwriting in secondary schools. Now they have an entitlement to receive tuition in this area.

In this issue of the *Handwriting Review*, the topic of handwriting speed receives wide coverage. This makes the issue of teaching handwriting in secondary schools highly relevant. If children are to achieve their maximum potential in public examinations, they need to be able to write legibly, but also to be able to write at length and still maintain speed.

The development of computer technology is becoming an interesting issue *vis a vis* handwriting. The paper by Sovik in this issue shows how computer technology can enhance our research techniques. It almost seems to be a contradiction in terms to be using state of the art late twentieth century technology to study a skill which is over two thousand years old! However, there is another issue about computers and handwriting in education. There are whisperings that handwriting may become obsolete. The reduction in the cost of "lap-top" computers and electronic note books is said to be sounding the death knell of handwriting for all but calligraphers. This must be a worrying trend. Computers are a wonderful aid to all aspects of education and beyond. This edition of the *Handwriting Review* has been produced using word processing packages, scanners, spell checkers etc. etc. However, computers can be a mixed blessing. Cunningham and Stanovich (1990) showed that computers are no substitute for handwriting when it comes to learning spellings in the early years of education. Spell checkers may help with the final drafting of materials, but they do not help a child to learn to produce the correct form automatically.

Katherine Perera, in her keynote address to the Australian Reading Association in 1993, pointed out that it is essential that we strive to increase the level of literacy in the world. It may be possible to conceive of a world where the need for literacy has been apparently superseded by interactive talking computers and where all our information comes from listening to television and other advanced technological wizardry. However, there will still be people in power who control the media and do the writing. The same can be said about handwriting in the foreseeable future. Not everyone has access to an electronic notebook, and while that is still the case, we need to ensure that all children have the opportunity to make their "voice" heard through writing - through **hand**writing.

This is the first issue of the *Handwriting Review* under the new editorship. Indeed, this is the first issue of the *Review* that has not been edited by Jean Alston. Tribute must be made to her hard work and dedication. Fortunately, stepping down from her editorial role has not meant that she has ceased to contribute to the *Handwriting Review*. It has been decided that the *Review* should be given Volume numbers to make it easier for people to search back numbers. Jean was responsible for editing the first 8 issues of the *Handwriting Review* and, though, they were not given volume numbers, it is only right and proper that the numbering of the *Review* should recognise her pioneering work. This issue is therefore Volume 9.

References

Cunningham, A. and Stanovich, K. (1990) Early spelling acquisition: Writing beats the computer. *Journal of Educational Psychology*, **82 (1)**, 159-162

Perera, K. (1993) Keynote address to the Australian Reading Association Conference, Melbourne, Australia

Rhona Stainthorp
The University of Reading

Handwriting Performance and GCSE Concessions

Michael Connor
Educational Psychologist, Surrey County Council

INTRODUCTION

In their report concerning special educational needs and examinations, Grant et al (1993) describe how, with few exceptions, examination syllabi are aimed at the majority of pupils. Pupils who experience any form of special educational need which may have an impact upon assessment are accommodated only at the end of the process, such that their needs are not integral to syllabus development and planning.

This implies the appropriacy of arranging concessions for examination organisation, but the authors highlight the lack of coherence in the range and applications of special facilities and conclude that the use of SEN categories may actually divert attention from the candidate's specific and individual needs and requirements.

While it is possible to gain accurate estimates of a student's reading accuracy, rate and comprehension, and of accuracy of spelling, it remains the case that:

a) rate, as well as accuracy of writing, is a significant factor in examination success.

b) there has been a lack of clear information about the level of performance which would be considered average for an age group, and, consequently, about the level that would represent a significant disadvantage in formal examinations.

There has, therefore, been inconsistency in the following areas:

1. Whether or not handwriting speed is measured at all when it comes to considering examination concessions.
2. The nature of the assessment.

3. The criterion level for significant disadvantage (in relation to other scores such as verbal ability, achievements in non-written tasks, etc.)
4. Whether or not a student should receive extra time for the writing of examinations, gain access to a portable word processor, or have answers transcribed.

Alston (1993) summarises research in this area and notes that the sample writing tasks have fallen somewhere along a range between two extremes. On the one hand there is repeated copying of some simple phrase; on the other, subject-generated free writing.

The first emphasises the purely "mechanical" rate of writing, while the second tries to provide a simulation of an examination setting. Not only has research varied in respect of the writing task, but also in terms of many other features such as the age of the subjects, the length of the time scale for the sample writing, the unit of measurement, etc.

Dutton (1989) has described how the earliest writing may be as slow as 1 or 1.5 words per minute at age 5+ years, but that rate may have risen to 18+ words by the age of 16 or 17 years. This would beg the question of how progress is influenced or how progress can be accelerated. It also begs the question of precisely what is being measured in a task involving a short sample of writing.

In sum, while noting the agreement set out by the Joint Council for the GCSE, that special arrangements are intended to remove as far as possible the impact of the disability on the student's performance, and enable the demonstration of actual attainment, it still needs to be decided how that impact can be assessed. This is all the more critical in the light of the reference by the Joint Council to the need to ensure that the special arrangements do not give the student an unfair advantage over all the other candidates in the same examination.

The Extra Time Concession

Sawyer (1993) surveyed the practice of examination boards and concluded that extra time is the most readily and frequently offered concession to students with specific difficulties. The spokespersons for the boards held that such a concession compensated for a student's difficulty while not going so far as to confer some actual advantage over other students, claiming that GCSE examinations are not setting out to test what can be written in a given time. However, this view appears questionable. The results from Sawyer's survey of the experience of students who had completed the examinations the previous year (drawn from VIth forms and acknowledged to represent the more scholastically minded students) suggest that time **is** a significant issue in examinations. For example, it was noted that 42% of the sample reported a failure to complete one or more papers in the time allowed and 27% did complete all the papers but argued that improvements would have been achieved if more time had been available. Within that first group (the 42%), the students' comments suggested that the time pressure applied to around one third of the examination papers, and that a wide subject range was involved, although History and Geography were most frequently cited as presenting difficulties of this kind.

The important implication from this is that extra time may indeed carry a very real advantage such that its availability should be considered only on the basis of clear and consistent criteria. A further implication includes the need for considering the extra time issue in the context of the particular examination, since any difficulty in writing speed *per se* may not impact equally across all the examinations, and for clarifying how precisely one is to assess handwriting rate.

Assessment

Comments from the Arkell Dyslexia Centre refer to 16-18 words per minutes as average for students at the stage of GCSE examinations, with the conclusion that a concession of extra time should be sought if a rate of less that 12 words per minute is observed. Assessment is based on one, or preferably two samples of free writing of 5 minutes duration in response to an exam-type question. However, it was stressed (Goedkoop 1989) that these conclusions are based on informal discussions with a number of educational psychologists, and that there is a need for reliable and normative data on writing speed.

The Surrey LEA working Group (1992) set out guidance for schools when applying for concessions and, in respect of writing, quoted a free writing rate of 17 (plus or minus 3) words per minute as an estimated average for 16 year olds.

However, these authors, too, accepted that this is only a rough guide in the absence of valid and reliable norms for expected writing speeds for senior school pupils, or even of an agreed system for carrying out an assessment.

Sawyer Francis and Knight (1992) point out that the arbitrariness of the assessment of handwriting rate has been heightened by an uncertainty whether speed should be calculated by the number of words (of varying lengths and complexity) or by the number of letters completed in a given time. There was also some question about the appropriate period of time that should be allowed for the assessment.

In their study, the authors used samples of students from upper, middle and lower ability bands in school year 10. Outcomes were as follows:

1. Marked differences were noted between the total of words completed under free writing and copying conditions. Minimal differences were observed among letter counts. Therefore, total number of letters was put forward as a preferred means of measuring output speed.
2. No significant differences were observed in the mean number of letters written per minute under test lengths of 2 or 3 minutes.
3. Ability level was seen as a powerful predictor of writing speed and output.

The implications drawn from this study were:

a) Given the variable of measured ability, it is necessary to ensure that concessions do reflect a specific weakness and not a global learning weakness. It may be necessary to gain data about mean writing rates among samples of students of different measured ability levels as a first step. The second step would involve examining an individual performance to highlight any discrepancy between the observed and the expected writing rate.
b) Short time limits for the sample writing task may not be adequate in seeking to predict written outputs in examination conditions. The test period should be extended to 15 minutes (or even longer) if one is to observe the onset of psychological or physiological fatigue, and the extent to which a student may be specifically disadvantaged.

Alston summarises results from various longitudinal studies, and quotes the pattern in subject-generated free writing presented in Table 1. The wide range of scores (albeit only quoted for the younger age groups) demonstrates the potentially misleading nature of an average and further begs the question of criterion levels for slow handwriting rate.

Still, on the issue of assessment, it may be argued that there is a lack of clear evidence to help determine the appropriacy of alternative recording methods in an examination. For example, Dutton quotes a rule of thumb from one examination board of 16 words per minute as the necessary writing speed for examination candidates. However, one might still ask whether the criterion level for additional support in the form of access to a portable word processor or to extra time (all else being equal) is 15, or 14, or 13, or n words per minute. Further, there is the complication in that writing speed may vary **during** the prolonged writing task as fatigue comes into play, or as ideas are exhausted, or as attention flags, or as whatever else that might happen does happen.

Table 1 Mean writing Speeds between the ages of 8 and 17 quoted by Alston (1993)

Age of Subject	Mean words p.m.	Range
8	3.75	1-11
9	5.65	1-15
10	6.00	2-16
11	7.65	3-20
13	12.50	
14	14.00	
15	16.00	
16	17.00	
17	18.50	

Dutton's own survey findings suggest that a 16 words per minute criterion would not be achieved by more than 50% of year 10 boys, although it could be a reasonable figure for girls. He cites a figure of 12 w.p.m. as a critical cut off point (at 2 sd below the mean).

It is important to note that, among boys, there appears still to be scope for maturation and improvement in writing performance from year 10 onward (and the general increase in writing speed across the age groups carries an implication for schools to continue to work on, and provide practice for, the mechanics of writing rather than to leave this behind once the secondary stage of schooling has been entered).

Following the work of Scardamalia, Bereiter and Goelman (1982), there is the further note of caution that slow writing is not simply a matter of "mechanics", but can interact with the quality or style of output in interfering with the flow of ideas, or in slowing down the compositional aspect of the mental process or inhibiting the short term memory "buffer".

This point is reinforced by Mason (1992) whose survey concluded that large numbers of pupils transferring to secondary schools would be unable to meet the criteria for English Attainment Targets 3a, 4a, and 5, e.g. *"Pupils should be able to begin to produce clear and legible joined-up writing"*. Difficulties appear to apply particularly to boys, and this underlines the existing evidence for sex differences in writing performance, with an implication for focusing attention upon senior pupils, especially boys, with a view to encouraging and developing fluent writing and rapid writing as necessary. In other words, the issue about concessions at age 16+ in the light of handwriting deficits should become redundant in all but a small number of special cases whose needs continue in spite of ongoing attention.

It is reported that the nature of writing difficulties can be wide ranging both extrinsic (in terms of the child's experiences) and intrinsic (in terms of some specific motor or visuo-motor disadvantage). In assessing whether handwriting *per se* is indicative of a need for modified examination arrangements, it must be remembered that limited written output may reflect poor planning, organisation, or knowledge of the subject matter as much as some mechanical disability. Charlton (1986) suggests that the main problems with examination output concern writing at speed and/or writing at length. Remedial actions might include:

a) Simple observation, or self analysis, to establish the best examples of work, and to determine the conditions that gave rise to them such that those conditions might be replicated.
b) Modifying seating arrangements, or the incline of desks, or the writing materials used.
c) Modifying the style or size of writing.
d) Constant practice including copying from a model, or tracing, or writing with eyes closed to develop kinaesthetic awareness.

There may be no universally applicable technique given the wide range of types of disability and experiences among children or young people with written-recording difficulties.

It is also accepted that, even if time and attention are made consistently available for the continued remediation of writing problems or for graded writing practice, there will continue to be cases of specific difficulty where it will be appropriate to seek examination concessions.

This leads back to the original question of how to identify those students who do merit special consideration because of a specific disability which will interfere with the demonstration of their knowledge of the subject, while ensuring that one does not shift the balance the other way in conferring upon those students some unfair advantage thus discriminating negatively against other non-disabled peers.

It was, therefore, planned to complete a further, albeit small scale, investigation which would take note of the outcomes from existing studies and focus attention upon the following issues:

1. Comparing and contrasting word count and letter count, and their respective means and standard deviations.

2. Sex differences in terms of observed output.

3. The interaction of written output with general ability measure.

4. The use of a relatively long time scale for the sample writing task.

5. The use of two types of task: one to involve subject generated material with pre-planning; the other to involve responding to a previously unseen examination question.

6. The issue of legibility should be included in the assessment, even if it may be difficult to gain any objective means of its measurement.

It was decided **not** to include a copying task on the grounds that such a task may involve quite different processes from those involved in subject-generated writing, such that outcomes of a copying task may have limited relevance and generalisability.

Subjects would be drawn from Year 11 pupils, at a point between their mock GCSE examinations and the actual examinations. Care would be taken to avoid any prior awareness of the purpose of the task, and to minimise risk of fatigue by setting the tasks on separate occasions with a time delay between presentations.

The goal of the investigation might be summed as the gaining of further and objective data thus to provide a context within which to examine individual performance, and to determine if a case exists for seeking examination concessions.

It was arranged that the tasks would be completed by students as part of their tutor group activities, and supervised by their own teachers, under the guidance of the support staff and the educational psychologist.

METHOD

Subjects

The pupil subjects were drawn from Year 11 of a mainstream comprehensive school serving a semi-rural area. All the pupils were involved at least initially in the exercise but a number of them were not represented in the final data. Reasons included their absence for one of the two tasks, some question whether they may have gone beyond the 20 minute time limit, and an inability on the part of the supervisors to match the 2 pieces of writing.

A total of 83 pupils formed the sample, 38 boys and 45 girls.

Procedure

The two tasks were carried out within English sets and supervised by the English teachers, under the guidance of the SEN Co-ordinator who, in turn, was given guide-lines. As a result of time-table demands or other commitments within this term, there was a prolonged delay of some 3 weeks between the administrations of Task One and Task Two.

In Task One, the subjects were invited to write on a topic of their choice. The suggestion was put to them that they might write on the subject "All about myself", and a few minutes were spent in sharing the kind of information that could be included. Subjects had the option to choose an alternative topic, and a number described their hobby or a recent event. What mattered was that subjects were able to write freely, uninterrupted by any need to spend time producing the content. When all subjects reported being confident to do so, a period of 20 minutes was allowed for the writing.

In Test Two, all subjects were simply presented with one printed question drawn from a past GCSE English paper and were allowed only a few moments to read the question before being invited to write their answers. Again 20 minutes were allowed.

The subjects were invited, at the end of the 20 minutes, to count both words and letters; and these totals were subject to checking by the supervising teachers, the SEN Co-ordinator, and the present writer.

Anonymity was assured, and the results for each of the two tasks were collated under the following headings: Pupil Number, Gender, Ability. Both letters and words were counted for each task.

The ability score was derived from the screening testing carried out on entry to school some 3.5 years earlier. From the AH4 Testing used, the Total Grade (A-E) was noted for each pupil. It is relevant to note that, according to the AH-Test normative data, this sample's pattern of ability scores was skewed towards the upper end, that is, while the A to E grades are predicted to follow a 10% 20% 40% 20% 10% distribution, the observed scores were not distributed in this balanced way. Instead, there were 29 pupils with grade A, 18 with grade B, 21 with grade C, 11 with grade D and 4 with grade E making 83 pupils in all.

In respect of legibility, all the scripts were examined by the experimenter and a teacher who rated them on a three point scale: A - Entirely legible; B - Legible with some difficulty such that reading flow is not smooth and C - Very difficult to read and illegible in parts. However, the two independent ratings placed the overwhelming majority of both sets of scripts into the A grade such that there was no scope for any analysis of this variable in interaction with other variables, further demonstrating that this pupil sample was indeed not fully representative of all pupil types/abilities.

RESULTS

The data for Task One is presented in Table 2 and for Task Two is presented in Table 3. Limiting the analysis to pupils who scored Grade A on the ability screening test, the mean words pre minute for the boys were 20.2 for Task One and 14.5 for Task Two. For the girls these figures were 19.0 for Task One and 11.4 for Task Two. In respect of Task Two, the difference between the means suggested that a significance level may have been reached, but analysis showed that the difference between sets of scores fell just short of the 5% level: i.e. while clearly there is a link between ability and output, there remains the marked difference in outcomes between Task One and Task Two.

Table 2. The mean number of words and letters written by the group during Task One

	Boys	Girls	Whole Group
Words per 20 minutes	350.55	375.44	364.05
Letters per 20 minutes	1430.53	1484.22	1459.64
Words p.m. (wpm)	17.53	18.77	18.20
	sd = 5.5	sd = 4.7	sd = 5.1
Letters p.m.(lpm)	71.53	74.21	72.98
Range of wpm	7-27.53	7.4-30.75	
Range of lpm	28.1-119.7	31.4-122.55	

Table 3. The mean number of words and letters written by the group during Task Two

	Boys	Girls	Whole Group
Words per 20 minutes	238.97	223.53	230.60
Letters per 20 minutes	1027.79	1001.76	1013.67
Words p.m.	11.95	11.18	11.53
	sd = 5.4	sd = 3.8	sd = 4.6
Letters p.m.	51.39	50.09	50.68
Range of wpm	3.25-21.65	5.4-22.65	
Range of lpm	15.4-97.75	23.6-112.95	

A correlation analysis was carried out on the data in Task One to compare output in terms of letters or of words. With N = 83, and the sum of the squared difference = 5194, the Spearman Correlation Coefficient was 0.9.

The outputs in terms of words written in Task One and in Task Two were compared. A correlated t-test showed that the difference in outputs was highly significant (t = 11+ when the 0.1% significance level is less than 4.) It is accepted that one might argue against the use of a t-test on the grounds that normal distribution of the scores may not be a fully justifiable assumption. Nevertheless, mere inspection of the scores demonstrates the considerable difference between the two tasks. For example, the mean difference between number of words produced in 20 minutes was 131 in favour of Task One; and in only 6 cases in 83 was the word output in task two greater than in task one (3 boys, 3 girls, ability grade 2A, 1B, 2C, 1E).

A trend analysis was completed in order to test the hypothesis that, overall, there would be greater written output as measured ability level rises.

Given the relatively small numbers in the screening test categories D and E, these were combined. This meant there were 29 pupils with grade A, 18 with grade B, 21 with grade C and 15 with grade D/E. With a comparison of the scores in terms of words produced in 20 minutes against ability category, the resulting Z-value from the use of Jonckheere's Analysis was 2.3 (1% significant) thus confirming that greater written output is linked to (measured) ability and that this trend is significant.

DISCUSSION

The results, in terms of actual writing speed, as measured in task one, are comparable to those quoted from previous research or surveys involving 16 year olds, viz. an overall average of 17.5 w.p.m. among boys and 18.7 w.p.m. among girls.

However, the difference in outcomes between the "free writing" and the examination-question tasks is striking, such that, if a given student produces a limited written response to a GCSE question, one should by no means necessarily attribute this to some difficulty in handwriting *per se* but might look instead at the interaction among factors like subject knowledge, examination-situation experience, planning/thinking time, and confidence, along with writing speed. Further, any measure of writing speed should involve the free-writing style such that this variable is not confounded with other variables.

Sex differences are discernible, albeit not to the extent that might have been predicted from earlier published findings. Girls appear a little more productive in the free-writing task (and this accords with existing research data) but it is interesting to note that the boys appear to take over a marginal advantage when it comes to the examination-type task and this advantage appears all the more at the upper end of the ability range. One might seek to explore whether there are differences in terms of confidence over launching into print, or of individual styles relating to planning the task, or whatever; in any event, the sex differences, albeit not reaching a significant level, are interesting and highlight the continuing need to work on examination technique and one should not be misled by the apparent facility demonstrated by girls in terms of spoken and written language .

To return to the main point, if one is to measure actual writing speed, unpolluted by such issues as thinking/planning time or by variations in the knowledge and competence to tackle a given question, then one would recommend the free writing task, i.e. the writing on some very familiar topic with opportunity afforded for pre-planning.

The considerable difference between the general level of outputs on the two tasks does highlight the significance of time allowed for completing answers, and underlines the need to be very specific about those pupils who should receive a time concession since it is likely that many pupils would benefit from further time to complete examination answers.

One notes the very close, although not absolute, correlation between letter and word counts. This being so, it would appear logical to use a word count in any further survey exercise given the considerably greater ease of gaining a word rather than a letter count, and given that adopting the more difficult procedure involved in a letter count would not significantly improve the data.

Table 4. The relationship of legibility gradings B and C to ability for each task.

		Task One B/C legibility	Task Two B/C legibility
Ability			
	A	3	4
	B	5	3
	C	3	3
	D	4	6
	E	0	3
Total		15	19

Reference has already been made to the matter of legibility, and one would reiterate that the "eyeball test" indicated no real scope for analysis, i.e. the 83 double sets of scripts were rated A - B - C for legibility as follows: For Task One there were 68 scripts rated A, 13 rated B and 2 rated C. For Task Two there were 64 scripts rated A, 16 rated B and 3 rated C. Table 4 shows the pattern of legibility gradings B and C with reference to the Ability levels of the pupils. This would suggest that one could not anticipate an ability/legibility pattern.

In respect of ability, there is a general trend which links greater (measured) ability to greater written output. However, one should stress that this is only a trend, albeit significant, since observations of the raw data demonstrate that the highest output scores in terms of words per minute are not consistently linked with the highest ability ratings. For example, the highest 20 "output" scores in Task One were linked to ability scores as follows: 9 grade A pupils, 5 grade B, 4 grade C, 1 grade 1D and 1 grade E.

CONCLUSIONS

1. Markedly different scores (word or letter counts) emerge from different writing tasks where the one emphasises free writing and involves minimal planning/thinking requirements, and the other involves an unseen GCSE question which will require thinking time or evoke some greater anxiety, or tap an area of specific, and perhaps, limited, knowledge. Thus, if written output is limited, this may not simply reflect slow writing speed *per se*.

2. To be meaningful, the writing task should not be too short, and the 20 minute time scale seems reasonable to ensure that one may tap the real range of writing speeds within a sample population of young people. For example, the marked Task One- Task Two discrepancy would not have been revealed if the time had been limited to 2 or 3 minutes. It is accepted that such a time scale may be perceived as unrealistic if all candidates for examination concessions, interviewed by an educational psychologist were so tested. However, there is no reason why group testing cannot be carried out, or why testing of this kind should not be completed in a school setting without the immediate involvement of an educational psychologist.

3. Although not directly relevant to the issue of examination concessions, one notes the general trend linking ability screening scores with written output rates; and the interaction, albeit not significant, between task demand and sex of subject. This may have ramifications for enhanced prior experience of examination settings and for continued work on examination skills and stress reduction. It is possible that girls may be particularly benefited from such activities.

4. While there is not a precise relationship between letter and word counts, the correlation is very high such that one would recommend adopting a word count as the standard measure given its relative simplicity. The use of a letter count would not appear, on this evidence, to provide any further meaningful data, but does provide increased scope for fatigue and errors on the part of the collator.

5. In seeking to highlight the candidate "at risk" in terms of handwriting speed, the mean" words per minute" scores (i.e. 17+ and 18+ for boys and girls) minus 1 sd would seem a reasonable point at which to pursue further evidence for a given child (i.e. ability level; verbal competence as judged by subject staff, etc.) in determining whether a case is to be made for examination concessions.

Nevertheless ....

6. Given the outcome of Task Two (the markedly lower output), one would support the view that many or most pupils would be able to improve performance as a result of further time, hence the need to target the pupils meriting extra time concessions very precisely.

Further, while 12 (boys) and 14 (girls) may be legitimately regarded as threshold word per minute levels at or below which to perceive pupils at risk, it would be appropriate to regard this current exercise as less than final and to extend the study to involve further samples of Year 11 pupils in order to gain a greater mix of socio-economic catchment areas and of pupil abilities/backgrounds.

Acknowledgements

The writer wishes to express grateful thanks to the pupils and staff of Glebelands School, Cranleigh, for their unstinting help in the implementation of this survey.

References

Alston, J. (1993) Assessing writing speeds. *Handwriting Review 1993*, 102-106.

Charlton, C. (1986) Handwriting problems; Non-teaching and teaching remedies. Unpublished Manuscript.

Dutton, K. (1989) Writing under examination conditions. *Scottish Education Department Regional Psychological Service.*

Goedkoop, G. (1989) Unpublished memo on the matter of assessment of writing speed. Helen Arkell Dyslexia Centre, Frensham, Surrey.

Grant, M., Came, F., Bowker, P. and Noble, J. (1993). Special educational needs and the GCSE Report submitted to S.A.E. Centre for Curriculum and Assessment studies. University of Bristol.

Joint Council for GCSE (1987) Standing agreement number 4. Provision for handicapped candidates. (Joint Council for GCSE 23-29 Marsh Street, Bristol BS 1 4BP).

Mason, R. (1992) Handwriting following transfer to secondary school. *Handwriting Review 1992*, 107-110.

Sawyer, C. (1993) Handwriting speed and special arrangements in GCSE *Handwriting Review 1993*, 7-9.

Sawyer, C., Francis, M. and Knight, E. (1992) Handwriting speed, SpLD, and the GCSE *Educational Psychology in Practice* **8(2),** 77-81.

Scardamalia, M, Bereiter C, and Goelman H (1982) The role of production factors in writing ability. In *What writers need to know*. New York: Academic Press, pp 173-209.

Surrey County Council (1992) Special arrangements in examinations for candidates with specific learning difficulties. Surrey E.P.S. and Surrey Literacy Support Service.

Assessing Writing Speeds and Output: Some Current Norms and Issues

Jean Alston
Educational Consultant

INTRODUCTION

Long standing readers of Handwriting Review will be aware of the continuing discussion about handwriting speeds and general written output, that has been recorded in this journal. The foregoing discussion has included Mason (1991), who examined handwriting speeds and other handwriting characteristics of first year secondary school pupils and Dutton (1992), who examined, through a standardised task, general written output of pupils in a Scottish Secondary School, in an attempt to establish a baseline for identifying candidates in need of special arrangements in 16+ examinations. Sawyer (1993), and Sawyer, Francis and Knight (1992), discussed the validity of writing speed measures and the equity, with regard to students in general, if certain pupils were to be given extra time. *Would not most pupils benefit from extra time?* is an important question for Sawyer.

The urgency to establish valid and reliable criteria through which to identify pupils in need of special arrangements for GCSE, General National Vocational Qualifications (GNVQ) and beyond, is increased by the greater contribution of examinations to 16+ awards. In earlier years, assessment could be entirely or partly through coursework assignments, and this became common practice prior to 1994. Examination Boards willing to accept special arrangements for pupils identified as having special needs, urge teachers to identify pupils likely to need those arrangements early in their educational careers. Implementation of the Code of Practice on the Identification and Assessment of Special Educational Needs (1994) means that pupils with learning difficulties can and should be identified from an early stage in school. Written output is an important vehicle through which needs and progress can be monitored. By "Written Output", I refer to a standardised piece of writing which can be compared with past and future performances, under the same writing conditions, as the pupil proceeds through school. A proposal for objective monitoring at the primary educational stage is reported by Alston (1992; 1994(1); 1994(2)). The 1994(2) research (Dyslexia Review, Vol 6, No 2) reported secondary school data from Cheshire and from the Island of Guernsey. Dutton (1992) reported similar data for Scottish secondary school pupils.

WHAT KIND OF ASSESSMENT?

Written output, of course, offers evidence of many aspects of progress or otherwise in writing skills. For example, it shows spelling errors and spelling characteristics, the degree to which conventions of punctuation have been understood and utilised, the status of the writer's written grammar and, at its perhaps simplest level, whether an efficient handwriting script is established Sawyer (1994) argues that written output, as such, samples too many skills, and gives too much information about the writer's performance, so that an essential element such as handwriting speed is not discernible. A timed symbol writing task, such as + O + O + O would, in his view, be most appropriate for assessing potential handwriting speeds. There is considerable merit in this proposal. However, for how long should a simple symbol repetition task be pursued, and is it a valid indicator of handwriting competence over an examination period of two hours or more?

PUPIL CHARACTERISTICS?

In much of the discussion recorded above, little attention has been paid to the nature of the pupils in need of assessment. Pupils vary enormously in their characteristics and needs, and rarely fall into precise categories. However, in current educational parlance there are those affected by specific learning difficulties (the dyslexics), and those affected by motor learning difficulties (the dyspraxics). In the area of handwriting, there are also pupils who have been badly taught and simply do not have handwriting competence and style. This third group of pupils, whilst usually showing no individual motor performance problems such as those experienced by dyspraxics, will often have a slower and less legible handwriting style which is not always easily distinguishable from characteristics shown by dyspraxic pupils. Only the implementation of handwriting teaching techniques to ameliorate superficial problems, and perhaps further assessment through tests such as the Test of Motor Impairment (TOMI) (Henderson and Sugden, 1992), can help us to differentiate the two.

A SOLUTION?

Established norms of written output, particularly suitable for identifying and assessing pupils with written language difficulties, are fully reported with means, standard deviations, and graphs on which written output of individual pupils can be recorded and monitored are reported by Alston (1994(2)). Although the parameters of written output are not precisely defined and are in need of an extensive research project if they are to be established, a framework for examining written output is established. "Written language difficulties", in this instance, can refer to generally low achieving pupils and/or to those with specific written language difficulties (dyslexics).

Handwriting speed and legibility are different matters, and the debate about what should be written and whether it should be copied or memorised as a short phrase or sentence (Alston 1992) continues. Sawyer's simple symbol copying task is a useful one, but is only likely to be utilised over a short period of writing time. The boredom engendered would surely mitigate against its validity as a handwriting output measure as copying time became extended.

Table 1. The mean writing speeds of a group of Primary school boys in Cheshire taken at yearly intervals between the ages of 7 years 10 months and 10 years 10 months

	7y 10m	8y 10m	9y 10m	10y 10m
Words per minute				
Mean	3.32	5.14	5.62	7.02
sd	1.56	2.54	1.92	3.16

Examples of data available in the extended article on written output (Alston 1994(2)), are presented in Table 1. The complete data includes a full range of data for Cheshire Junior School pupils, written performance of first year pupils attending a Cheshire Comprehensive School, and for first and fifth year pupils attending La Mare De Carteret Secondary

Modern School in Guernsey. A validity study, comparing results for a written output task with those on a mock GCSE examination paper complete the research data. The complete report is available in Dyslexia Review Vol 6, No 2.

References

Alston, J. (1992) Assessing Writing Speeds. *Handwriting Review 1992,* 102-106.

Alston, J. (1994(1)) Christopher: a boy with inordinate handwriting and spelling difficulties. Handwriting Review.

Alston, J. (1994(2)) Written Output and Writing Speeds. Dyslexia Review, Vol 6, No 2. Available from: The Dyslexia Institute, 133 Gresham Road, Staines, Middlesex, TW18 2AJ.

Department for Education (1994) Code of Practice on the identification and Assessment of Special Educational Needs. Department for Education, Great Smith Street, Westminster, London, SWIP 3BT.

Dutton, K. P. (1992) Writing under Examination Conditions: Establishing a baseline. *Handwriting Review 1992,* 80-101.

Henderson, S. E., Sugden, D. (1992) Movement ABC, including Test of Motor Impairment ('TOMI). The Psychological Corporation, Foots Cray High Street, Sidcup, Kent, DA14 5HP.

Sawyer, C. (1993) Handwriting Speed and Special Arrangements in GCSE. *Handwriting Review 1993,* 7-9.

Sawyer, C. E., Francis, M. E., Knight, E. (1992) Handwriting Speed, Specific Learning Difficulties and the GCSE. *Educational Psychology in Practice,* **8(2),** 77-81. Reprinted in the *Handwriting Review 1993.*

Sawyer, C. E. (1994) Handwriting speed and special arrangements for examinations: what are the issues? Lecture at University of London Institute of Education.

To What Extent is Writing Speed Related to Other Aspects of Handwriting?

Nils Sovik
Professor of Education, University of Trondheim, Norway

INTRODUCTION

Various aspects of the development of children's manual writing skill are stated by objectives for the handwriting curricula and instruction. For instance, their writing behaviour should be 'healthy' (correct placement of the paper, good penhold, etc.), and the writing should be performed easily and fluently, with speed and accuracy (legibility) in accordance with the expected norms. However, Sassoon, Nimmo-Smith and Wing (1986); Sovik (1993), and Mojet (1991) have found that teachers usually pay little attention to writing speed when evaluating children's handwriting performances, even though a growing interest for process and speed variables in writing now can be observed among researchers as well as some practitioners (Sawyer, Francis and Knight, 1992; Van Galen, 1993).

If the objectives of speed and physiological convenience (easy and well co-ordinated movements) in handwriting should be considered as important as legibility, the relationships between the process and product variables call upon further empirical research. Although significant correlations are found between speed and accuracy (legibility) in writing when people write with a slow, 'normal' speed (Sovik, 1979; Sovik, Arntzen and Teulings, 1982), practice seems to indicate that the relationship is gradually changed into a zero correlation (no relation) or often a negative correlation (inverted relation) between the same variables whenever an individual is stressed to write fast.

To date, relatively few studies have been carried out to investigate systematically the relations between writing velocity (speed), co-ordination of writing movements/rhythm and the quality (accuracy) of the writing product (Mojet, 1991; Sovik et al., 1982). In consequence, we were concerned with the following problems in the current study:

    1. To investigate the relationship between writing velocity and the co-ordination of writing movements/writing rhythm (process variables).

    2. To study the relationship between writing velocity and the quality, i.e. accuracy/deformations of letters, of the writing product under various test conditions.

METHOD

Design and Subjects (students)

An experimental study was designed with students grouped equally on good vs. poor writers, in order to examine the effects of various writing speed conditions and writing quality (factors) on the dependent variables in question.

Sixteen 15 year old children were chosen as subjects for the study. The sampling procedure was as follows: First, specimens of 142 children's functional handwriting performances (work-books used in languages) were collected, rated and classified into good (above average) and poor (below average) writing products by two trained raters. Second, eight children (based on the specimens) were sampled randomly among children classified as good writers, whereas another eight children were sampled among those in the group of poor writers.

Task, Tests, and Procedure

Two series of tasks were used for the experiment: 1) a sentence consisting of 11 words, and 2) 11 meaningful words with no internal relations (no sentence) which were written separately, (one at a time with breaks between them). The words in series 2 were matched in length and structure with the words in series 1. Before the experiment started, the students had learnt the two series of tasks by heart.

In addition the two series of words used as tasks in the experiment, two visuo-motor tests, Southern California Motor Accuracy Test by A. J.

Ayres, and Visual-Motor Integration Test by K. E. Beery and N. A. Buktenica, were administered to the students.

Writing took place with A4 paper superimposed on a digitizing tablet equipped with an electronic pen, a system which was controlled by a microcomputer. A combined system of three cameras provided an efficient video recording of the penholds and finger/hand-movements of the students. When doing the experimental tasks students (tested individually) used their personal writing style (cursive writing). They did not receive a display of the tasks, but the experimenter (E) always told the students which alternative of writing speed that was to be followed in performing a task.

These were the alternatives:
1. To write with a slow, ('normal') speed.
2. To write with a relatively fast, ('normal') speed.
3. To write with a maximum speed (only used for series 1 - the sentence).

When students did the writing tests, data were stored on disk for later reviewing and analyses. The absolute writing velocity was derived from these data, and the velocity curve, as a function of time, was displayed on a graphical terminal. The velocity curve(s) together with the test item and total writing time could be plotted on a sheet of paper by means of a plotter.

Measures and Scoring of Data

Students' writing specimens were collected and scored in accordance with a 5 point scale for accuracy by two persons already trained in this work. The time (speed) used in writing each of the tasks was scored by the computer.

Models were developed for every item by an adult who had a high quality of writing rhythm. These models of writing rhythm were used when students' performances were rated. The rhythm-score of a writing performance was calculated as an average score based on the similarity between the trajectory of the model and those of the test-items, the score of even/uneven trajectory, and the number and lengths of interruptions in the trajectory.

The percentage of letter-deformations in the students' writing specimens was decided in accordance with the criteria of accuracy (legibility). Furthermore, when students did the various tests their writing behaviour was systematically observed, and ratings of: a) the grip of the pen, b) the degree of upright body, and c) overt behaviour of co-ordination of muscles in fingers/hand/wrist were carried out by E and his assistant (A) according to 5 point scales. As students were video recorded during the testing sessions, the observations/ratings of their writing behaviour could later be checked.

RESULTS

Observational data regarding students' grip of the pen and the position of arms and body, indicated that only a minority used a 'hygienical' (good) grip/position. The majority practised a rather awkward grip and hand position while doing the writing tasks, and there were more good writers (quality of writing products) than poor writers who used such an awkward penhold.

Intercorrelations were calculated between variables used in the study, and significant inter-relationships were found between grip, position of body, and co-ordination of fingers/wrist during students' writing process. However, no significant correlations occurred between the co-ordination variable and any other variables under study, except for 1) time spent per letter and 2) writing accuracy when students wrote with a slow, normal speed. In both cases, the relationships were negative, which demonstrates that students with a fairly good co-ordination of their writing movements wrote faster than others (and vice versa), whereas the same students as a group seemed to produce writing of a rather low standard of accuracy.

Data based on observations of students' co-ordination of writing movements were further analysed in a so-called repeated measurement design, with the two first speed conditions, (slow normal and fast normal speed in writing a sentence), as within-subject variable and between subjects as factors. Table 1 presents the results of this analysis of variance. Whereas no significant difference was revealed for the within-subject effect, the average co-ordination score of the group of poor writers was found to be significantly higher than the one disclosed for the comparable group. No interactions occurred.

Table 1. Means of ANOVA with speed conditions and writing skill used as factors. Dependent measure/rating: Co-ordination of fingers/hand/wrist in children's writing.

Writing Skill	Sentence: Slow 'normal'	Sentence: Fast 'normal'
Above Average - N=8	2.13	2.00
Below Average - N=8	3.63	3.25

Concerning the general measure of students' hand motor control, the Southern California Motor Accuracy Test, correlated significantly with students' 1) fast, normal speed, and 2) rhythm in fast, normal speed when writing separate words. However, no significant correlation was obtained between The Visual-Motor-Integration Test (copying figures) and any other variables used in the present study.

Table 2 contains figures (average scores) from an analysis of variance with writing rhythm used as dependent measure. In this analysis two different speed conditions were used: slow normal and fast and normal writing speed, but data were collected and analysed from two different sets of tasks (sentence and separate words) under the category fast, normal speed. A significant main effect (speed conditions) was found with regard to students' writing rhythm. The highest average score for rhythm was obtained by slow, normal speed. However, the related correlation data between rhythm and writing time were not significant.

Table 2. Mean of ANOVA with speed conditions and writing skill used as factors. Dependent measures: writing rhythm.

Writing Skill	Sentence: Slow normal	Sentence: Fast normal	Sep. words: Fast normal
Above average N=8	2.53	1.58	2.44
Below average N=8	2.43	1.95	2.15

Furthermore, variables representing rhythm did not correlate substantially with the measure of students' writing accuracy, but a significant correlation appeared between rhythm measured in slow, normal speed and rhythm in fast, normal writing of separate words, which indicated stability in students' motor control and pattern of rhythm when students were writing different tasks, provided that a normal writing speed could be used. Finally, it should be added that a difference was found between good and poor writers concerning rhythm.

Table 3. Means of ANOVA with speed conditions and writing skill used as factors. Dependent measure: writing accuracy.

Writing Skill	Sentence: Slow normal	Sentence: Fast normal	Sep. words: Fast normal	Sentence: Max: speed
Above average N=8	4.13	2.88	3.09	2.00
Below average N=8	2.00	1.25	2.07	1.00

Figures in Table 3 indicate a gradual decrease in average accuracy from slow, normal to fast, normal, and further to maximum writing speed in using the same tasks, (standard sentence), for testing. When writing separate words with fast, normal speed the means (average scores) of students' accuracy scores lie between the corresponding means for the first and second speed level. In other words, a significant speed effect on writing accuracy was revealed. The trend is the same for both categories of writers, and related correlational data supported the findings. The results should be viewed in relation to the data reported next, with reference to the percentages of the letter deformations in students' writing performances. Prior to this, it should be made clear that a significant difference between the two groups of students, in favour of the good writers, was found and presented in Table 3.

Table 4. Means of ANOVA with speed conditions and writing skill used as factors. Dependent measure: percentage of letter deformations in the children's writing.

Writing Skill	Sentence: Slow normal	Sentence: Fast normal
Above average N=8	29.90	48.28
Below average N=8	47.08	68.75

Table 4 presents results concerning the average percentage of letter deformations in the writing performances of the students under two experimental conditions: sentence with slow, normal speed and sentence with fast, normal speed. In general, the percentages of letter deformations are rather high, and a significant difference between slow and fast speed condition was found, with a higher rate of deformations for fast writing. Similarly, considerably more deformations showed up among the poor than the good writers.

DISCUSSION AND CONCLUSIONS

In the present study, it was confirmed that students could regulate their writing speed, and it was observed that such changes in writing velocity could take place even though the majority of the students wrote with a rather awkward grip of the pen (a cramped grip). The results indicated that more students chosen as good writers with regard to writing accuracy had awkward penhold/positions of hand/arm than had the comparable group, and it should be noted that poor writers as a group always wrote significantly faster than the good writers. A reasonable explanation for this result may be found in the close relationship that seems to exist between a good penhold and well co-ordinated writing movements, and further between co-ordinated writing movements and fast writing. Teachers responsible for instruction in handwriting should be fully aware of these relations that seem to exist between children's penholds, the co-ordination of their writing movements, and their conditions for writing with a relatively high speed.

The analyses of writing rhythm resulted in favour of 'slow, normal writing speed', i.e. in general, fast writing leads to a more firm or sometimes cramped grip of the writing instrument, that further seems to affect the co-ordination of the movements and the writing rhythm in a negative way. The conclusion was supported by the correlational data in the study. In future research, one therefore ought to study more thoroughly whether children at different stages in primary and junior school are pressed too heavily regarding writing speed. There are reasons to believe that many children are often forced to write too fast, thus passing the 'threshold' (capacity) for writing smoothly with good co-ordinations of writing movements (Sovik, 1993; Van Galen, 1993).

In the current study, we were also concerned with the relationship between writing velocity and the quality of the writing product. First, our empirical data showed that the quality of students' accuracy-scores in writing was much reduced when their writing speed was altered from slow to fast, and further to maximum speed. But the significant intercorrelations found among accuracy-scores under different speed conditions verified the theory of stability to be expected for the variable accuracy (legibility) (Mojet, 1991; Sovik, 1993). Second, the frequency of letter-deteriorations increased by faster writing performance which can be considered as a parallel finding to research on the relation between speed and accuracy in writing. The skilled writing movements are complex and often difficult to carry out when fast performance is required. Such characteristics tend to occur more frequently in graphic performance of difficult letters or letter-combinations (Meulenbroek, 1989; Sovik, Flem and Karlsdottir, 1989). It follows that a great many letters will be deformed, and the general accuracy-scores will decrease, whenever a child is forced to write with a relatively rapid speed. The findings should be taken into account in future planning of writing curriculum and instruction.

References

Ayres, A. J. (1964) *Southern California Motor Accuracy Test.* Los Angeles: Western Psychological Services.

Beery, K. E. and Buktenica, N. A. (1967) *Developmental Test of Visual Motor Integration.* Chicago: Follett.

Meulenbroek, R. G. J. (1989) *The study of handwriting production: Educational and developmental aspects.* Nijmegen: PhD thesis, NICI, University of Nijmegen.

Mojet, J. (1991) Characteristics of the developing handwriting skill in elementary school. In J. Wann, A. M. Wing, and N. Sovik (eds.) *Development of graphic skills.* Cambridge: Academic Press, pp. 53-76.

Sassoon, R., Nimmo-Smith, I., and Wing, A. M. (1986) An analysis of children's penholds. In H. R. S. Kao, G. P. Van Galen, and R. Hoosain (eds.) *Graphonomics: Contemporary research in handwriting.* Amsterdam: North-Holland, pp. 93-106.

Sawyer, C. E., Francis, M. E., and Knight, E. (1992) Handwriting speed, specific learning difficulties and the GCSE. *Educational Psychology in Practice.* **8, (2),** 77-81.

Sovik, N. (1979) Some instructional parameters related to children's copying performance. *Visible Language,* **XIII, (3),** 314-330.

Sovik, N. (1993) Development of children's writing performance: Some educational implications. In A. F. Kalverboer, B. Hopkins, and R. Geuze (eds.) *Motor development in early and later childhood: Longitudinal approaches.* ESF. Cambridge: University Press. pp. 229-246.

Sovik, N., Arntzen, O., and Teulings, H. L. (1982) Interactions among overt process parameters in handwriting motion and related graphic production. *Journal of Human Movement Studies.* **8,** 103-122.

Sovik, N., Flem, A., and Karlsdottir, R. (1989) Contextual factors and writing performance of 'normal' and dysgraphic children. In R. Plamondon, C. Y. Suen, and M. L. Simner (eds.) *Computer recognition and human production of handwriting.* Singapore: World Scientific. pp. 333-347.

Van Galen, G. P. (1993) Handwriting: A developmental perspective. In A. L. Kalverboer, B. Hopkins, and R. Geuze (eds.) *Motor development in early and later childhood.* ESF. Cambridge: University Press. pp.217-228.

Pencils with Triangular Barrels: How First Year Pupils and Their Teachers View Them

Sheila E. Henderson
Department of Educational Psychology and Special Educational Needs (EPSEN), Institute of Education, London University
Jean Alston
Educational Consultant
Louise Robertson
EPSEN, Institute of Education, London University.

INTRODUCTION

The teaching of handwriting is now a compulsory component of the National Curriculum. The final version of the Secretary of State's deliberations are now in schools and the recommendation that *"... pupils be taught to hold a pencil conformably in order to develop a legible style that follows the conventions of written English"* is an integral part of the programme of study at Key Stage 1. As the subject of handwriting has been virtually ignored for more than a decade it now means that teachers who have had relatively little training in teaching the subject will be anxiously searching for good teaching materials.

Materials for teaching handwriting can be divided into two broad categories. The first includes those concerned with what the child actually puts on paper, ranging from schemes for the beginning writer to schemes for teaching the advanced skills required for calligraphy as an art form (see Alston, 1993, for a review). The second category includes the materials the writer requires to produce the written trace, such as writing surfaces, paper, pencils, pens etc. As far as this latter category is concerned, it is frequently the case that teachers make decisions about what they buy for their pupils without any knowledge of the ergonomic factors at issue.

Focusing specifically on the implements used to write with, there is no doubt that the physical characteristics of the implement have an effect on the way we write (e.g. Sassoon, 1983). A round, slippery barrelled pen, for example, is hard to hold and forces the writer to grip the pen with excessive force. This in turn leads to excessive pressure on the writing surface (Herrick and Otto, 1961), a reduction in fluency of movement while writing and in the longer term, writer's cramp (Sassoon, 1983). Young children are currently presented with a whole range of writing instruments from the short fat infant pencil to full-size felt tip pens. Sometimes, different instruments are recommended for different graphic skills, at other times the children are given no guide-lines at all on the use of particular instruments.

There is a general belief among teachers that the development of a dynamic tripod grip is desirable for the skill of handwriting. This belief has some basis in the literature on the development of grip in young children (e.g. Connolly and Elliott, 1972; Rosenbloom and Horton, 1971; Saida and Myashita, 1979; Erhardt, 1974; Keogh and Sugden, 1985; Ziviani, 1987). Very briefly, what these studies show is that the way a child holds an implement for drawing or writing changes systematically with age (see figure 1).

Initially - at about the age of 12-18 months - children tend to hold the implement in a palmar grasp with all four digits curled around it. In this case the whole arm is used to move the pencil and neither the arm nor the wrist is in contact with the paper. They then move from this position through a grip called a distal pronate grip, an incomplete tripod and various versions of a static tripod grip (e.g. 3 digits on the barrel). Finally, a dynamic tripod grip may emerge anywhere between the ages of four and a half and six. There are two sources of variation present in these data. First, all of the "grips" described in the studies represent a category of hand configuration rather than a highly specific configuration. In other words, each category encompasses minor variations in things like the position of the wrist, the location of the hand on the implement, the amount of flexion in the first digit and so on. Second, there is variation in the rate at which children pass through the stages with not all reaching the final stage of using the dynamic tripod.

(1) Palmar grasp

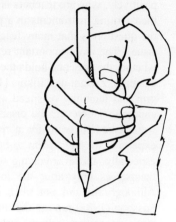

(2) Incomplete tripod

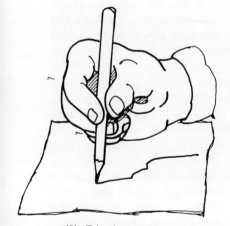

(3) Tripod posture

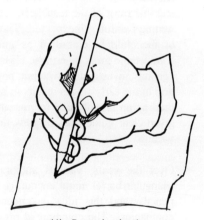

(4) Dynamic tripod

One question that emerges in the educational context in relation to this literature, is this - why is there still uncertainty about whether teachers should <u>insist</u> on children using a dynamic tripod grip, or, put more positively, why are teachers uncertain about <u>teaching</u> their children to hold their writing instruments in a particular way. The uninteresting answer to the question is that many teachers have never been asked to consider the issue. The more important reason is that there is some uncertainty about whether the way one holds the implement affects the finished product. For example, Ziviani and Elkins (1986) found no relationship between type of grip and legibility or speed of writing in a group of 218 primary school children. However, the disadvantage of this study was that the children were asked to write for a relatively short period of time. What most experts in the field seem to believe is that disadvantages of "odd" grips - especially those involving extreme tension in the fingers - reveal themselves only after the individual has been writing for some time. Although she did not tie her observations directly to grip or posture, Sassoon (1983) reports that most of the teenagers she spoke to in a New York secondary school disliked writing and found it painful. This observation has recently found empirical support in a study of fifteen year old children classified as "good" or "poor" writers by Sovik, Arntzen, and Karlsdottir (1993) who found that quality of writing did correlate with grip and that most of the teenagers with poor grips complained that they found writing painful. Unexpectedly, however, this study also showed that more of the children classified as **good** writers wrote slowly and had less comfortable grips than those classified as **poor** writers. Unfortunately, no one has investigated whether paying particular attention to posture and grip in the early stages results in better and faster writing later on. Clearly, there is an urgent need for research on this topic so that teachers can be given clear guide-lines on how to proceed in the early stages of teaching writing.

Over the years, various authors have suggested that a pencil with a triangular barrel might encourage children to adopt a "good" grip on their pencils, and this idea has been pursued by a number of commercial companies. The commercial products take two forms. Some companies have produced a proper pencil, others have produced a sleeve which slips over a pencil of any shape. Both of these products are already popular with special needs teachers and therapists who use them with children and adults who have an unconventional and/or uncomfortable grip, which seems to be affecting their writing.

As might be expected from the preceding comments, however, very little research on the efficacy of triangular instruments has been undertaken. In fact, one of the most extensive pieces of research to date, was done by Jean Alston, one of the authors of this report (Alston, 1986). In this project, Alston compared eight year old children's use of the triangular pencils made by Learning Development Aids with their use of the hexagonal pencils they commonly used in school. As far as choice was concerned 64% of children wished to retain the original hexagonal school pencil and 36% wanted the triangular pencils. The study also revealed that a change of pencil did not affect the way the children held their pencils at all. When scores were awarded for conventionality or appropriateness of pencil grip, higher marks were awarded when pupils were writing with the pencil barrel that was most appropriate for their already established pencil grip. In other words, the pupils seemed to know which barrel suited their grip and selected accordingly. What we have learned from this study, of course, is that a short term change of pencil by itself will not affect an already established grip - whether the addition of instruction would alter this outcome is an interesting question.

Some time ago, we were commissioned by Berol PLC to conduct an exploratory study of the use of triangular pencils by children just beginning writing. As so little was known about what characteristics an infant school pencil should have we opted for 2 triangular shaped pencils of different widths (length identical). These were to be compared with the pencils currently used in the schools participating in the project.

There were various questions we could have asked about the value of these pencils, but we selected three as the most useful to begin with. The first concerned the children's attitude to the new pencils. Young children are strongly influenced by their own preferences for the objects around them. This is likely to be as true for the pencils they use as for their toys at home. If they do find an object attractive they will use it; if they do not they will reject it. An important element of this project therefore was to determine whether the children we were studying chose the new pencils of their own accord. Our second question concerned the teachers' opinions of the pencils. As teachers are the decision makers when it comes to purchasing writing instruments, their view is just as important as the children's. Our final question concerned the way the children held the pencils they were using and its effect on their graphic output (i.e. writing and copying).

METHOD

Subjects

Sixty children aged between 4.5 and 5.8 years participated in the project - about half were boys and half were girls. The children were all in their reception year of schooling. They attended three Primary Schools, two in North Staffordshire and one in South London. The London school was in an urban, densely populated district. The Staffordshire schools were more rural.

Materials

The materials used included 2 prototype triangular shaped pencils supplied to us by the Berol company and the schools' own choice of pencil. The latter were School 1: NES Arnold Hefty hexagonal; School 2: Berol Alphex Soft ; School 3: Berol Graduate HB. The triangular pencils were put in the pencil container with an equal number of new school pencils at the appropriate time. There was always one of each type of pencil for every child in the class and all of the pencils were new. They were kept sharpened throughout the project.

Procedure

The project began with the researchers making themselves and their photographers known to the teachers and children. It was explained to the children that some new writing pencils would be brought for them to try out and that they would have their photographs taken on several occasions. Any further questions about the project were answered by the children's teachers who simply explained that the visitors were trying out some new pencils and wanted to know whether the children liked them or not.

The project proceeded in three distinct phases and data was collected over a six week period as follows:

Phase one - establishing the status quo:
The data collected at this stage represented the base line from which all other judgements were made. The children were first tested using the pencil they were familiar with (this, of course, varied from school to school as described above). Each child completed the following tasks:
- Writing their names: Each child was asked to write his/her name on a line ruled across the lower half of an A4 sheet of plain white paper

presented in "landscape" format. The instruction was " Write your name on the line. If you cannot write all of it write as much as you can".

- Copying: Each subject was asked to copy the phrase "cat and dog" which was written in lower case print on a line ruled in the upper half of an A4 sheet of plain white paper, also presented with the long edge facing the child. A line was ruled on the lower half of the same sheet of paper for them to write on. The instruction was "Copy the words on this page onto the line below. Do as much as you can".

- Photographs: One of the tables was moved from its usual position in the classroom to allow the photographer to move around it freely. The children were seated two at a time, on opposite sides of the table and at diagonally opposite ends so that two photographs of each child could be taken whilst they were completing the writing and copying samples in their booklet. The photographer took a picture of each child's whole body posture and then a close up of their lower arm and hand position, on each of the three occasions. These photographs were side on, from the child's left hand side so their fingers, hands, upper body and posture were clearly visible. (The photographs would be taken from the right hand side for a left handed subject).

Phase two - the children's choice of instrument:
This phase of the project lasted for just over two weeks and included the following data collection:

- Recording of the children's preferences among the old and new pencils: After the children had been shown the new writing pencils, the class teacher and helper were asked to quietly observe and note down at three intervals each day which shape pencil each subject was using if they were writing at that time. This was done each school day for two weeks. (We attempted to minimise the possible effect of the adults on the subject's choice by allowing the children to collect the pencil they wanted from the writing materials table themselves and they were not told anything of the pencil monitoring process).

- Collection of writing and copying samples and taking of photographs. After the two week period had elapsed the tasks described above were presented to the children in the same way as before.

- A discussion of what pencil the children would like to keep for the next few weeks and why: This was done with each subject on a one to one basis in the classroom. A small table, facing the wall was used to minimise the visual distractions and allow the child's verbal responses to be more clearly heard. The responses were written down as they were given, after stating to the child "I'm writing down what you say to me on this piece of paper". An example of each type of pencil was on the table during the interview.

Phase three - longer term record of performance:
After each child had noted which pencil he/she wished to write with, this was then marked with his/her name and used consistently for all writing tasks for a period of four weeks. The following data was then gathered:
- Collection of writing and copying samples, and taking of photographs as described above.
- Another discussion of whether they had liked their chosen pencil and why.
- Completion of the teacher questionnaire.

In summary, all data was collected during normal in-class sessions. Times were selected that did not clash with out-of-classroom activities such as assemblies, P.E. etc. Disruption and unfamiliarity were minimised as far as possible - even the photographers soon became popular visitors.

RESULTS AND DISCUSSION

The results obtained from this project so far will be discussed under three headings - the children's views of the pencils, the teachers' views of the pencils and the effect of the pencils on grip. Before presenting these results, three points are relevant.

First, our analyses revealed no differences at all attributable to either age or gender. The age range of the children involved was rather narrow so this finding is not unexpected. We had no particular expectations of differences between boys and girls and made no observations that suggested differences were present. We, therefore, make no further mention of these variables.

Second we felt that it was difficult to evaluate the differences that emerged in relation to the two triangular pencils. With the wisdom of hindsight it would have been useful to measure the size of the children's hands to see whether those who chose the smaller pencil were choosing an instrument that suited their hand size. As we did not do this we suggest that more attention should be paid to the choice of overall shape rather than to the specific pencil chosen.

Third, it might be useful to note that in one school, a number of problems, unrelated to our project, arose which placed demands on the teacher's time and resulted in a distinct reduction in enthusiasm over the six week period.

The children's views of their pencils

During the two-week period of <u>free choice</u> when both the existing school pencil and the two triangular pencils were available to the children - the school pencil was selected 31% of the time and the triangular pencils 69% of the time.

Breaking down the choice of triangular pencils according to the two options:
- the large version was selected 43% of the time
- the small version was selected 26% of the time.

During this period, of course, some children changed pencils frequently.

The pupils were then asked which of the three pencils <u>they wished to keep for the next few weeks</u>:
- 23% chose to keep the school pencil
- 77% chose to keep a triangular one (60% large, 17% small).

The children who chose to write with the <u>large triangular pencil</u> after two weeks gave the following sorts of reasons for their preference:
> ...*because it's nice*
> ...*don't know*
> ... *that feels skinny* [small triangular pencil], *that feels skinny* [school pencil] *and that feels fat* [large triangular pencil]
> ...*I just did like it*
> ...*because I like it*
> ...*because it's fat*
> ...*because it's new*
> ...*because it just came*
> ... *because it's fat and it's a different shape*
> ...*because you can draw with it and write with it and Camella says she can take one home*
> ...*because it's more bigger and I don't like 'cos I'm five*
> · ...*the red ones* [school pencil] *keep on hurting people*
> ...*because it's got a triangle and a dot* [the barrel shape and lead showing at the end]

> *...because it was big. I used to like these as well* [school pencil]
> *...because it's got a pointy end and a pattern down the edge*
> *...because Mrs. E. brought it*
> *...because it's big and it's brown*
> *...because these ones roll over* [school pencil] *but these ones don't* [large triangular]
> *...because it's big and nice and fat, it's easy to hold*
> *...because it's got lines on it.*

The children who chose the <u>small triangular pencil</u> gave the following reasons for their choice:

> *...because I didn't like the fat one of these ones* [triangular pencils]
> *...because it's thinner*
> *...because it's new*
> *...because it was comfortable*

Of the children who chose the school pencil, some preferred it because they liked the colour or some other visual feature whilst others gave mixed responses saying they liked one pencil but choosing another.

After a further four-week period of using the pencil of their choice:
- 41% preferred the school pencil
- 59% preferred a triangular one (47% large, 12% small).

However, when our problem school was removed from this analysis
- 13% preferred a school pencil.
- 77% preferred a triangular one.

The children then gave the following sorts of reasons for their preferences:

Big triangular
> *...I like the fat one*
> *...because it's big*
> *...because it's big and I like triangles, big triangles*
> *...because it's got lines and sharpy end and a triangle*
> *...because it was comfortable*
> *...because it's fat and it's the colour*
> *...because it's bigger than all the others I thought*
> *...because it had lots of lines*
> *...because it's nice and big*

> *...because the little one* [small triangular] *I not like, I like this
> one* [touched large triangular] *because it's my favourite one
> ...because I like it in the wood colours
> ...because it is easier to hold*

Small triangular

> *...because it's little and it's not fat
> ...because they was new
> ...because it's nice and thin. I don't like the fat ones
> ...because it's got stripes on it*

School pencil

> *...because it's nice and warm and hard
> ...because it's red
> ...because this one's* [school pencil] *got words on it and
> diamonds and it's a thick pen.*

Taken together, these findings suggest that our experimental triangular pencils were more popular with the children concerned than those they had been using previously. Although strictly speaking, it is not legitimate to simply ignore the school that found itself less able to cope with the demands of the project, our observation was that the teacher had lost enthusiasm and therefore, might be conveying that feeling to her pupils. Certainly, when we examined the data from the remaining two schools (which contained 45 of the original sample of 60 children) the picture obtained was much more consistent. Throughout the six week period approximately three quarters of the children concerned chose to write with one of the two triangular pencil and seemed to like them.

The question of what to conclude from the children's comments is difficult. We considered the possibility of asking them to make comparative statements about the relative merits of the various options but decided that this was a task five year olds might find too difficult. What we obtained, therefore, were very general comments about the visual appearance of the pencils rather than their writing quality. In our view, however, these comments are valuable - they indicate that children pay attention to shape and are able to express their likes and dislikes albeit in a crude way.

The teachers' views of the pencils

The responses to the teachers' questionnaire show that teachers who liked the pencils are in a majority. In general, the large pencil is more popular than the small one but the option to paint the pencil is not popular. However, it must also be noted that each of the three teachers thought the pencils would only be suitable some of their pupils. Why they thought this is not at all clear - unless they had been strongly influenced by Sassoon's emphasis on giving young children a choice of writing implement. Clearly, this issue is something which requires further investigation.

The effect of the pencils on the children's grip and graphic output:

Although we have now scored all of the handwriting samples, we have not yet begun to investigate the relationships between these variables and pencil grip. In this paper, therefore, we can only describe our preliminary findings on how the children held the pencils while writing.

The close-up photographs of each child's grip with the different pencils, taken during the six-week study period were examined by a number of trained professionals including both teachers and therapists. Using some rather crude criteria, we classified the grips of the children into the following categories - dynamic tripod, static tripod, incomplete tripod (i.e. thumb wrapped over the index finger) and "odd/ unclassifiable".
The results were as follows:

dynamic tripod	32%
static tripod	23%
incomplete tripod	33%
odd	12%

What this means, of course, is that approximately fifty percent of this sample of children had already acquired either a dynamic or a static tripod grip after only two terms in school. The implication of this finding, is that if triangular pencils are to be properly evaluated as **facilitators** of grip development then we need to begin in the nursery with children who have progressed less far.

What we did try to do, however, was examine the grips of those children who were still in a state of transition to see whether their grips varied more with type of pencil. We can also examine later whether these are also the children whose graphic output is least mature. From doing this very informally, however, it was not our impression that many of the children's grips changed when they changed pencils. Perhaps it is unreasonable to expect that the pencil by itself will facilitate change. It may be necessary for the teacher to use the pencil as one part of her strategy for encouraging children to develop a comfortable writing grip.

SUMMARY and RECOMMENDATIONS

The objective of this project was to provide the Berol company with information which they could use as part of their decision about the manufacture of a triangular pencil. In view of the fact that there were already competitors on the market, our initial discussions included debate about whether there were disadvantages of currently available instruments which the Berol company could rectify. Two points were noted (1) that the sharp edges on existing pencils were undesirable and (2) that highly painted pencils were difficult to hold. The pencils produced for the current project attended primarily to these features. In this study, we have shown that both children in infant schools and their teachers liked the basic parameters of the pencil and seemed to find them attractive. So far, however, we have failed to show that the pencils directly affected the children's grip on the pencil or how they well they wrote but we are still examining this question. It is, however, our tentative conclusion that too many of our subjects had already acquired a tripod grip for any effects to be demonstrable. If we were able to show that a triangular pencil helped children acquire a good grip before entering infant school, we believe that teachers would then continue to use them as a way of maintaining good practice.

OUTCOME

Following the submission of an extended version of this paper report, the Berol company produced the Handhugger range of pencils with the following technical specifications: rounded triangular barrel (with overall side length of approximately 1 cm); "wood" constructed from wood waste flour bonded together with resin; non-slip matt finish; medium/thick lead which cannot break inside the casing, available in both black and colour; will not split when chewed!

References

Alston, J. (1986) The effects of pencil barrel shape and pupil barrel preference on hold or grip in 8 year olds. *British Journal of Occupational Therapy*, **49**, 32-35.

Alston, J. (1993) Handwriting schemes, models and materials: a survey. In J Alston (ed) *The Handwriting Review 1993*, 78-113.

Connolly, K. & Elliott, J (1972) The evolution and ontogeny of hand function. In N .B. Jones (ed) *Ethological studies of child behaviour*. Cambridge : Cambridge University Press.

Erhardt, R P (1974) Sequential levels in the development of prehension. *American Journal of Occupational Therapy*, **28**, 592-596.

Herrick, V. E. & Otto, W. (1961) Pressure on point and barrel of a writing instrument. *Journal of Experimental Education*, **2**, 215-230.

Keogh, J. & Sugden, D. A. (1985) *Movement Skill Development*. New York: Macmillan.

Rosenbloom, L. & Horton, M. E. The maturation of prehension in young children. *Developmental Medicine and Child Neurology*, **13**, 3-8.

Saida Y. & Myashita, M. (1979) The development of fine motor skills in children: manipulation of a pencil in young children aged 2 to 6 years old. *Journal of Human Movement Studies*, **5**, 104-113.

Sassoon, R. (1983) *A practical Guide to the teaching of Handwriting*. London: Thames and Hudson.

Sovik, N. Arntzen, O., Karlsdottir, R. (1993) Relationships between writing speed and some other parameters in handwriting. *Journal of Human Movement studies*, **25**, 133-150.

Ziviani, J. (1987) Pencil grasp and manipulation. In J Alston & J. Taylor (eds) *Handwriting : Theory, Research and Practice*. London: Routledge.

Ziviani, J & Elkins J. (1986) The effect of pencil grip on handwriting speed and legibility. *Educational Review*, **38**, 3.

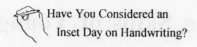

Have You Considered an
Inset Day on Handwriting?

The Handwriting Interest Group has access to a
number of professionals who speak on a range of
topics related to handwriting.

◆We Can Help To Organise An Inset Day◆

Examples of talks which can be provided:

National Curriculum Update - It's Implications

A Handwriting Policy for Your School

Criteria for Selecting a Handwriting Model

Identification of Handwriting Difficulties

Keyboarding Skills - Why? When? How?

Practical Advise on Teaching Handwriting

Helping Left-Handed Children

Contact: B. Scheib, 1 D'Abernon Drive, Cobham, Surrey, KT11 3JE

The Handwriting Skills of Young Early Readers.

Di Hughes
*Department of Education Studies and Management,
The University of Reading*

INTRODUCTION

This paper presents the preliminary findings of a longitudinal, three year study monitoring the reading and writing development of a group of children identified as being able to read fluently prior to entry to Year R, and a matched group of control children. All aspects of reading and writing are being studied, but only those data relating to handwriting will be discussed here.

Although writing development involves more than the acquisition of handwriting and spelling rules (Czerniewska, 1992), for the youngest children in school a greater proportion of their mental energy when writing is directed towards spelling and handwriting. Wray, Bloom and Hall (1989) note the physical demands imposed by the manipulation of the writing instrument in the earliest stages and Meek states :

> *" To learn to write always involves practice with a tool which has to be brought under control so that the writer can concentrate on putting together the message rather than forming the signs. "* Meek (1991), p.19.

The National Curriculum (1989) acknowledged that handwriting and spelling are likely to make greater demands during the early primary years, by considering these two aspects separately from levels one to four - Attainment Targets (AT) 4 and 5 - but combining them as a single Attainment Target - Presentation - beyond this level. However, in the 1994 National Curriculum Orders (for implementation in Key Stage 1 from August 1995), all aspects of writing are included in a single attainment target - AT3, Writing. In the programmes of study, spelling and handwriting are considered as separate Key Skills in Key Stages 1-4. In Key Stage 1 specific note is made of the importance of forming letters conventionally, with regularity of size and shape of letters and uniformity of spacing of letters and words.

Handwriting has become an area of increasing concern to early years teachers. Peel and Bell (1994) stress that it is important for a school to discuss a handwriting policy to obviate the need for children to change styles as they mature. Their statement is supported by Noad (1990) and Sassoon (1993) who argue that because changes take place in the nervous system when a new motor pattern, such as letter formation, is learned, incorrect motor patterns once established or automated will be difficult to correct. Augur (1990) suggested that such incorrect patterns needed to be "unlearned" before proper movements can be taught.

Many schools are now introducing a cursive style of writing from Year R and several of the children in the present study are or will be attending such schools. Some of the main arguments for teaching cursive script from the beginning are that it follows on from free scribble movements, correct letter formation is ensured, words are produced as distinct entities and spelling is helped, (Cripps and Cox, 1989). However many children will have had experience of writing prior to starting formal schooling and thus it could be assumed that some "incorrect motor patterns" will already be established. Alston and Taylor (1987) detail the types of pre-school experimentation of children. Weinberger (1993) found that all the children she studied had access to writing materials and were using these before their entry into nursery school. Even Bauers and Nicholls (1986) who state that most children do not attempt to learn to write until they come to school, recognise that some children are able to produce letter shapes

> *"..before they have been given any formal instruction by the teacher"* p.139.

Over the last decade there has been a great increase in commercial packages concerned with writing that are available to parents and an increasing number of children arrive in school with considerable experience of writing (see parental comments below).

Cripps and Cox acknowledge this early experience but feel that children should not be asked to record with a pencil and paper before correct letter formation has been taught. They suggest alternative ways of recording. Cripps and Cox cite Sassoon (1983) as evidence that young children may have sufficient motor control for joining letters. Sassoon states that, although pre-school children should not be pushed into trying to form letters before their hand-eye co-ordination is sufficiently developed,

> *"flowing, separate letters are quite within the capabilities of 5 year olds and lead naturally into cursive as the child matures. "*
> Sassoon (1983) p.11.

However, work by Laszlo (1986) indicates that for some 5 year olds this may not be so. Laszlo believes that it is kinaesthesis *"..the modality which signals information relevant to the state of muscles and joints"* which is crucial to the acquisition and performance of skilled movements including writing. In their study of 491 children, Laszlo and Bairstow (1983) found that thirty three percent of six to seven year olds showed only a rudimentary level of kinaesthetic processing ability. Laszlo and Bairstow (1985) therefore question whether training in fine pencil and paper skills starts too early for some children. Garton and Pratt (1989) caution schools against holding unreasonably high expectations of children's writing abilities They feel that some children who may find handwriting difficult will gain little from copying letters but should nevertheless be encouraged to write for enjoyment.

THE CURRENT STUDY

Seventeen children able to read fluently prior to entry to Year R, (the pre-school reader group - PSR) and fifteen control children (the C group) were identified (Stainthorp and Hughes, 1995). At a mean chronological age of 5 years the PSR group had a mean reading age of 8 years 7 months (range 7 years 10 months to 10 years 10 months) on the British Ability Scale (BAS) Word Reading Scale and a mean accuracy score of 8 years 4 months on the Neale Analysis of Reading Ability (revised) (NARA). At a mean chronological age of 5 years 2 months the C group had a mean reading age - BAS Word Reading - of 5 years 6 months - range 5 years - 6 years 5 months. There was no significant difference between the two groups on the British Picture Vocabulary Scale (BPVS). The mean BPVS score for the PSR group was 80.5 (sd 14.4) and for the C group was 75.8 (sd 13.6). A t test comparing the two groups gave a t value of t(16)= 1.16, p=0.26.

A wide range of standardised and non-standardised assessments have been carried out and will be repeated annually. Those particularly relevant to the handwriting task are:

1. BAS Copying.
2. Letter knowledge
3. Concepts About Print (CAP), Clay (1985).

In addition, information from parental questionnaires indicated that all the children in the study had experience of writing prior to school entry. Examples of their comments are given below.

> *"...could write her name unaided at 3 and followed dots to write short thank-you letters."*

> At 3 years 10 months *".....suddenly decided she could write and wrote the full alphabet."*

> *"He enjoyed an Usborne Big Book for learning to write letters and numbers at about 3."*

> *"She is very proud of her writing and has always been praised for it - even if you couldn't understand it."*

> *"At the age of 3 he could write his name."*

> *"At 2 she started using pencil and paper and copying letters and drawing pictures."*

> At 3 years *"....he was doing his own 'pretending' writing."*

ASSESSMENT RESULTS

BAS Copying

In this assessment the child is asked to copy up to nineteen designs of increasing complexity - from a single vertical line to a circle, a triangle, a series of letter like forms and designs combining straight and curved lines. The assessment was carried out with 17 of the PSR group and 15 of the C group between 1 and 23 days before the handwriting task. Raw scores were analysed as 3 children scored above the 99th percentile. The PSR group obtained a mean raw score of 12.5 (sd 3.0) and the C group a mean raw score of 11.8 (sd 3.3). A t test comparing the groups gave a t value of t(30)=0.60, p=0.55. There was no significant difference between the groups.

Of the thirteen children, (7 PSR and 6 C), who scored at or above the 95th percentile, nine, (5 PSR and 4 C), were using a dynamic tripod grip and five were not. Of the two children who scored below the 50th percentile, one. a PSR, had unresolved laterality and one , from the C group, used a dynamic tripod grip.

Letter Knowledge

There was a significant difference between the two groups in their ability to give letter names and letter sounds when shown printed lower case letters - Sassoon Infant font, 40 pt.

Eleven of the PSR group knew the names of all the letters, four knew 25 and two knew 22. None of the C group knew all the letter names and there was a wide range of 0-22.

There was greater variation in the PSR groups ability to give letter sounds, four children knew all the sounds and there was a range of 17-26. None of the C group knew all the sounds and there was a range of 0-24.

Mann-Whitney tests showed that the PSR group had significantly greater knowledge of letter names (U = 1/U'=271, associated probability, p<0.0001) and letter sounds (U =29.5/U'=242.5, associated probability, p < = 0.0001)

Between two days and four months after giving letter names and sounds orally, the children were asked to write letter forms when given the letter name and, separately, when given the most common letter sound, e.g. /z/ for "s". The large differences in timing occurred as the giving of letter names and sounds was used as part of the screening procedure in identifying the PSR group) . Upper or lower case letters were accepted and scoring was lenient with reversals and primitive letter shapes being awarded a score as long as there was a clear differentiation between letters. Ambiguities were not scored.

Eleven of the PSR group were able to write all the letters when given their name (eight of these were children who had been able to give all letter names), three wrote 25 letters, one wrote 23 and two wrote 19. None of the C group could write all letters by name and there was a range of 0-24. Nine of the children in the C group were able to write more names than they were able to give, including one child who wrote 24 letters but five days earlier had given the names of only 3.

Similar results were obtained for writing letters by sound. Three of the PSR group could write all letters when given their sound with a range of 19-25 for the remainder. One of the C group wrote all letters, with a range of 1-25 for the rest.

Mann-Whitney tests showed a significant difference between the two groups both for writing letters by name ($U = 17.5/U' = 237.5$, associated probability, $p < 0.0001$) and by sound ($U = 45.5/U' = 209.5$, associated probability, $p=0.0015$).

Thirteen letters were designated as having a clearly differentiated upper case form - A N J B R E H T G Q L D I. On examining the correct responses for these letters it was found that the PSR group produced 31% (name) and 27% (sound) as upper case and the C group 61% (name) and 36% (sound) as upper case.

Concepts About Print

The mean raw score for the PSR group was 19.3 and for the C group 11.9. The maximum score for this test is 24. A t test showed a significant difference between the two groups ($t(31)=8.71$, $p<0.0001$).

Responses to items 15 - meaning of a question mark, 21- letter concept, 22 - word concept, and 24 - capital letter concept were thought to be of particular relevance to the handwriting task, as they were features represented in the handwriting task. Clay (reported in 1985), gives the ages at which 50% of average children pass these particular items as:

> Item 15 - 6 years 6 months
> Item 21 - 5 years 6 months
> Item 22 - 6 years 0 months
> Item 24 - 6 years 6 months

Table 1 shows the scores obtained by the two groups of children in this study.

Table 1: The number of children in each group who were able to achieve success on items 15, 21, 22 and 24 of the Concepts About Print Test

	Concepts About Print Items			
	Item 15 ? mark	Item 21 Word	Item 22 Letter	Item 24 Capital
PSR Group N=17	11	14	15	5
C Group N=15	3	13	8	1

A t test comparing the performance of the two groups gave a t value of t(30) =2.80, p < .01, the PSR group were significantly better than the C group on these items, but at a lower probability level than for the complete test. It is interesting that although all the PSR group were reading well above a 6 year 6 month level, only four passed all of these items

The Handwriting Task

This was administered on an individual basis to 17 of the PSR group - 11 girls and 6 boys - and 13 of the C group - 7 girls and 6 boys. At the time of the assessment 14 children, (8 PSR and 6 C), were in their first or second term in a Year R class and 16 children were attending state or private nursery classes or playgroups, their chronological ages ranged from 4 year 7 months to 5 years 6 months (see Table 2).

The children were asked to copy the sentence:

Can you see the dog with the ball?

This was printed on a single line using Sassoon Infant font 30 pt. All the PSR group and one of the C group were able to read the sentence, it was read to the rest of the C group, the reader pointing to the words as she read them.

Table 2 The ages of the children and their length of time in school when the handwriting task was administered

	Age Level		
	Oldest	Middle	Youngest
	5y 3m - 5y 6m	4y 11m - 5y 2m	4y 7m - 4y 10m
Schooling			
2nd term YrR	5 PSR, 4C		
1st term YrR	2 PSR, 1C		1PSR
Nusy/playgrp		3PSR, 3C	6PSR, 5C

Each child was given a sheet of A4 paper presented horizontally with a single line drawn across the paper halfway down, and a round HB pencil. The children were told *"You can write here* (pointing to the line) *or here* (pointing above the line)".

Laterality and pencil grip

One child, PSR group, was left handed and one, PSR, displayed unresolved laterality.

Nineteen children, (10 PSR and 9 C), were using a dynamic tripod grip. Seven children, (5 PSR and 2 C), held the pencil between the thumb and first two fingers, resting the pencil on the third finger. One right handed child, PSR, held the pencil between the thumb and three fingers and at times used an inverted hand posture (c.f. Ziviani, 1987, p.33). Two children (both C group) varied their grip. The child with unresolved laterality held the pencil between the thumb and three fingers in both his right and left hand, when using his left hand he held the pencil further from the tip. It is interesting to note that, in a free writing task, approximately six months later, this child was consistently using his left hand holding the pencil between his thumb and first two fingers and resting it on the third finger. Only one other child had modified the grip to a dynamic tripod.

The Baseline

Eighteen children, (10 PSR and 8 C), made a definite attempt to start writing on the baseline. Their first letter lay on or across the baseline or had its base within 2mm of the line. School experience appeared to have little bearing on their decision as eight of these children were in Year R and ten at nursery/playgroups.

Thirteen children, (7 PSR and 6 C), used more than one line for the eight words, one PSR required three lines to complete the sentence! One child from C group, wrote the words she could not fit on the first line above the other words. Only one child, PSR, split a word between lines. He had shown an understanding of "word" in the CAP test. All the children maintained a left to right convention. Clay (1975) gives examples of children who continue their writing right to left, once they reach the end of a line

Although, ideally, deviation of each letter from the base line should have been measured (see Alston and Taylor, 1987, p.166), this was logistically impossible, requiring 750 measurements. Therefore, as a crude measure of a child's ability to write in a straight line, the maximum deviation from the baseline was measured. Where a child had not started on the line a horizontal line was drawn beneath the first letter.

Table 3: The maximum deviation from the baseline, measured in mm, made by the children in each group.

	Maximum deviation				
	1-4 mm	5-9mm	10-14 mm	15-20 mm	20+mm
PSR Group					
N=17	4	7	2	1	3
C Group					
N=13	-	3	4	2	4

Table 3 shows that the majority of the children found writing in a straight line difficult, with sixteen children placing at least one letter 10mm or more from the baseline. A t test comparing the performance of the two groups gave a t value of t(28) = 1.73, p = 0.09. There was no significant difference between the groups.

Table 4 shows the maximum deviation from the baseline when the whole sample was divided into children who started writing on the line and those who did not. A t test comparing these two groups gave a t value of t(28) = -1.33, p=0.19. Thus, for these young children, the use of a line made little difference to their ability to write straight across a page. However Pasternicki (1987) discusses research findings which show that the use of lined paper facilitates legible handwriting, he suggests that beginner writers should be introduced to lined paper *"..at the earliest opportunity"*.

Table 4: Table showing the maximum deviation from the baseline in mm depending on whether the children chose to use a line or not.

	Maximum deviation				
	1-4 mm	5-9mm	10-14 mm	15-20 mm	20+mm
Using a line. N=18	4	7	3	1	3
Not using a line. N=12	-	3	3	2	4

Gaps between words and gaps between letters

There was a great variation in the gaps left between words and between letters both within individuals and across the groups as a whole. As with the deviation from the baseline, it was not practically possible to measure the gap between each letter and between each word. Therefore, the smallest and largest gaps were measured, giving four measurements for each child (smallest and largest gap between words and smallest and largest gap between letters). The size of the difference between the smallest and largest gaps should indicate the regularity of spacing, and the smallest measurements indicate whether sufficient space was being left between letters and between words. Additionally, by comparing the two sets of measurements, it was possible to determine if a child was leaving larger gaps between words than between letters.

Seventeen children, (7 PSR and 10 C), left gaps of less than 2 mm between words, nine children, (6 PSR and 3 C), had gaps greater than 15 mm. The smallest range was 3 mm (from 3-6 mm) and the largest was 27 mm (from 0-22 mm). Thirteen children had ranges greater than 10 mm. They found it difficult to space their words with any degree of regularity. Most children, 26 of the total sample, had at least one instance where a gap between words was smaller than a gap between letters, see Figure 1. However four children showed no such overlap.

Figure 1: Examples of gaps between words being smaller than gaps between letters.

As a subjective measure of spacing a number of observers, both professionally trained and not, were asked to judge the number of gaps between words for each sample (maximum 7). They were advised to allot one mark for line breaks as long as a word was not split between lines.

Table 5: The numbers of gaps left between words by the children in each group.

	Number of gaps							
	0	1	2	3	4	5	6	7
PSR Group N=17	1	2	1	0	2	3	2	5
C Group N=13	0	3	2	2	1	2	1	2

A t test comparing the performance of the two groups gave a t value of $t(28) = 1.22$, $p = 0.23$. There was no significant difference between the groups.

All four children who showed no overlap between their ranges for words and for letters, scored seven. The remaining three children who scored seven had an overlap between ranges of only 1 mm. All of these children passed item 22, concept of word, on the CAP test. However, the six children, (3 PSR and 4 C), who scored zero or one also passed this item. The child with unresolved laterality scored one and the left handed child scored two. They were obscuring their own writing for at least part of the task. During the free writing task, six months later, it was suggested to these children that they might like to reposition their paper so that it slanted both declined!

Letter representation

Twenty three children, (15 PSR and 8 C), made some attempt to represent all twenty six letters. In the PSR group, one child repeated a complete word having realised that she did not have room for the final letter on the preceding line, one child omitted "the" and one omitted "ee" of "see". In the C group, four children omitted one letter and one child omitted two. For such young children the rate of omission appears low, particularly as many of them were not marking word boundaries. Ten children from each group represented the question mark, of these, seven of the PSR group and two of the C group had passed item 15, concept of question mark, on the

CAP test. It would appear that, for some of the C group, inclusion of the question mark was not related to their understanding of its use.

None of the children differentiated the upper case C at the beginning of the sentence by making it taller than all their other mid-zone letters, although five of the PSR group and one C group had passed item twenty four, capital letter, on the CAP test. Seven children, 6 PSR and 1 C group, replaced between one and three lower case letters with the appropriate upper case, L A T N B H. All these children had produced the upper case allograph when writing letters to name and sound. The translation from lower to upper case could indicate that the children were processing the sentence to be copied at a more central level and retrieving the upper case allograph from the graphemic motor pattern store (Ellis, 1982).

Letter formation

All the children were able to demonstrate that they were aware of how at least one letter was produced conventionally. One of the C group children however produced a large number of primitive forms, often using several strokes for a letter (see Figure 2). He was one of the middle group of children attending a playgroup. Thirteen of the children, (5 PSR and 8 C), although showing some awareness of conventional letter formation, were inconsistent in their ability to form letters conventionally and demonstrated some lack of pencil control (see Figure 3).

Letters were often produced with two or more strokes and nine of the children made letter reversals or produced a similar letter in place of the target - "o" for "a" (see Figure 4). Eight of these children were in the youngest, three in the middle and two in the oldest group. Two of the thirteen were in their second term of Year R and two in their first term.

The remaining sixteen children, 12 PSR and 4 C group, formed the majority of their letters conventionally and showed no reversals (see figure 5). Ten of these children were in the oldest group, two in the middle age range and four the youngest. Eight were in their second term of Year R, two were in their first term and six children had not yet started school. It is however, important to note that, in some education authorities, all the children in the sample could have been at school.

Figure 2: Examples of primitive letter formation.

n
a
d
w

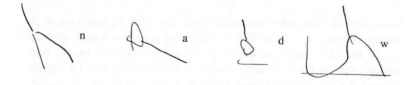

Figure 3: Examples of conventional and unconventional letter formation from 3 children.

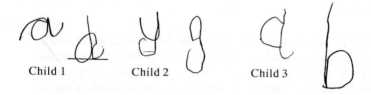

Child 1
Child 2
Child 3

Figure 4: Examples of letter reversals and letter formation using 2 or more strokes.

g
y
e
a
w

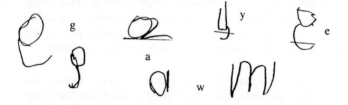

Figure 5: Example of conventional letter formation.

canyousee the dog with the ball

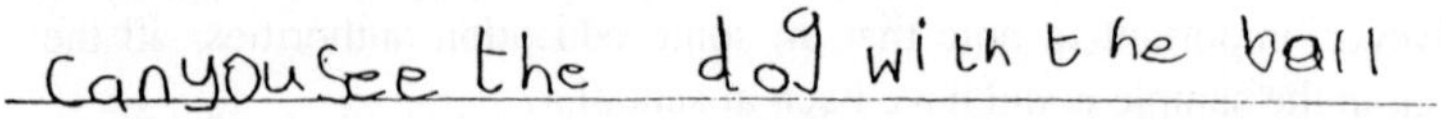

Letter size and alignment

There was considerable variation in the height of letters produced, from 3 mm to 50 mm. In order to provide a measure of each child's ability to produce letters of a regular size, four measurements were made: 1) shortest mid-zone letters (13); 2) tallest mid-zone letters (13); 3) shortest letters with ascenders (7) and 4) tallest letters with ascenders (7). From this information the following can be deduced:

1. Regularity of size of mid-zone letters (the smaller the range, the greater the regularity).
2. Regularity of size of letters with ascenders.
3. Ability to make a distinction in size between mid-zone and letters with ascenders.

For example, one of the C group children had ranges of 5-8 mm and 7-8 mm: both her mid-zone letters and her letters with ascenders were of a regular size, but some of the former were the same height as the latter.

Table 6 shows the difference in height between the shortest and tallest mid-zone letters. Nine children, (6 PSR and 3C), showed a variation of 5 mm or less. Their letters were approaching a uniform size. However, four children, (3 PSR and 1 C), showed a variation of 16 mm or more.

Table 6. The numbers of children in each group producing mid-zone letters at varying ranges.

Difference between shortest and tallest letter (in mm).

	0-5mm	6-10mm	11-15mm	16-20mm	20+mm
PSR Group N=17	6	5	3	1	2
C Group N=13	3	3	6	0	1

Table 7 shows the difference in height between the shortest and tallest letter with an ascender. eight children showed a variation of 5 mm or less, seven of whom (5 PSR and 2 C) had shown the least variation in their mid-zone letters. Six children showed a variation of 16 mm or more, only two of whom (1 PSR and 1C), had shown the greatest variation in their mid-zone letters.

Table 7. The numbers of children in each group producing letters with ascenders of varying ranges

Difference between shortest and tallest letter (in mm).

	0-5mm	6-10mm	11-15mm	16-20mm	20+mm
PSR Group					
N=17	5	8	0	2	2
C Group					
N=13	3	5	3	0	2

T tests carried out on the data gave a t value of t(28) = -0.17, p= 0.86, for mid-zone letters and t(28) = -0.17, p= 0.86 for letters with ascenders. There was therefore no significant difference between the groups.

The seven children with the lowest range for both letter types could be said to be producing letters of a regular size for both the mid-zone letters and letters with ascenders. however, all the children showed some overlap in sizes. They produced at least one mid-zone letter that was the same height or taller than their tallest mid-zone letter.

The size of the two letters with descenders was not measured, but only two children placed the descender below the baseline.

SUMMARY

For some children starting school, their areas of greatest need in handwriting may appear obvious.

Eleven children, (7 PSR and 4 C), were not using a dynamic tripod grip. Six of these children, however, were forming most letters conventionally. Sassoon (1993) cautions against changing any unconventional grip unnecessarily. The progress of these children will need to be monitored to ensure that grip does not affect later proficiency by causing fatigue or decreasing writing speed (Ziviani, 1987). The remaining five children demonstrated varying degrees of difficulty in letter formation and control of letter size. For two of the PSR group, the child with unresolved laterality and the child with inverted hand posture, achieving a grip which would give them greater control of their writing implement would appear to be a priority.

The C group child who produced a large number of primitive letter forms, (see figure 2) also found copying non-letter forms relatively difficult. He scored at the 44th percentile on the BAS. He was already using a dynamic tripod grip and an analysis of his ability to produce writing patterns, as detailed by Alston and Taylor (1988), would be helpful should his incorrect motor patterns persist.

However, for those children, starting school already able to form most letters conventionally their areas of need are not so easily determined.

One child showed little deviation from the base line, she placed descenders correctly and was beginning to show appropriate gaps between words and letters. However, the difference between her smallest and largest mid-zone letters was 25 mm and all her letters with ascenders were shorter than her tallest mid-zone letter.

The left handed PSR group child showed little deviation from the baseline. She had a variation of only 4 mm for her mid-zone letters and she made some of her letters with ascenders taller than her mid-zone letters. However, she used six upper case letters and failed to mark gaps between words consistently (see Figure 6).

Figure 6: Example of the writing of a left-handed child.

Therefore, even when young children are able to form letters conventionally, controlling size and relative size of letters, their orientation on a page and regularising gaps between letters and words remain as possible areas requiring further support. Sciriha (1990) indicated similar findings in her group of older children (mean age 94.78 months) and Clark (1976) remarked that some of the young fluent readers in her study showed average or below average standards of handwriting.

It will be interesting to compare this initial analysis with data collected when the children are in Year 1 and Year 2.

References

Alston, J. and Taylor, J. (eds) (1987) *Handwriting: Theory, research and practice.* Beckenham: Croom Helm.

Alston, J and Taylor, J. (1988) *The hand writing file,* 2nd *edition,* Wisbech: Learning Development Aids.

Augur, J. (1990) Dyslexia - Have we got the teaching right? In P. Pinsent (ed) *Children with literacy difficulties.* London: David Fulton. pp 52-65

Bauers, A. and Nicholls, J. (1986) Early writing. In A. Wilkinson (ed) *The writing of writing.* Milton Keynes: Open University Press.pp 134-157.

Clark, M. (1976) Y*oung Fluent Readers.* London: Heinemann

Clay, M. M. (1975) *What did I write?* Auckland: Heinemann Educational Books.

Clay, M .M. (1985) *The early detection of reading difficulties, 3rd edition.* Auckland: Heinemann.

Cripps, C. and Cox, R. (1989) *Joining the ABC: How and why hand writing and spelling should be taught together.* Wisbech: Learning Development Aids.

Czerniewska, P. (1992) *Learning about writing: The early years.* Oxford: Blackwell .

DES (1989) *English in the National Curriculum.* London: HMSO.

DfE (1994) *The National Curriculum Orders.* London: HMSO.

Dunn, L. M., Whetton, C. and Pintilie, D. (1982) *The British Picture Vocabulary Scale.* Windsor: NFER-NELSON.

Elliot, C. D., Murray, D. J. and Pearson, L. S. (1983) *The British Ability Scales.* Windsor: NFER.

Ellis, A. W. (1982) Spelling and writing (and reading and speaking). In A. W. Ellis (ed) *Normality and pathology in cognitive functions.* London: Academic Press. pp 113-46.

Garton, A. and Pratt, C. (1989) *Learning to be literate: The development of spoken and written language.* Oxford: Blackwell.

Laszlo, J. (1986) Development of perceptual motor abilities in children 5 years to adults. In C. Pratt, A. Garton, W. Tunmer and A. Nesdale (eds) *Research issues in child development.* Sydney: Allen and Unwin. pp 137-144.

Laszlo, J. and Bairstow, P. (1983) Kinaesthesis: Its measurement, training and relationship to motor control. *Quarterly Journal of Experimental Psychology,* **35A**, pp 411-421.

Laszlo, J. and Bairstow, P. (1985) *Perceptual-motor behaviour: Developmental assessment and therapy.* London: Holt, Reinhart and Winston.

Meek, M. (1991) *On being literate.* London: The Bodley Head.

Neale, M. D. (1989) *Neale Analysis of Reading Ability- Revised British Edition.* Windsor: NFER-NELSON.

Noad, B. (1990) Perceptual motor problems related to literacy. In P. Pinsent (ed) *Children with literacy difficulties.* London: David Fulton. pp 88-98.

Pasternicki, J. (1987) Paper for writing: Research and recommendations. In J. Alston and J. Taylor (eds) *Handwriting: Theory, research and practice.* Beckenham: Croom Helm. pp 68-80.

Peel, R. and Bell, M. (1994) *The primary language leader's book.* London: David Fulton.

Sassoon, R. (1983) *The practical guide to children's handwriting.* London: Thames and Hudson

Sassoon, R. (1993) Handwriting. In R. Beard (ed) *Teaching literacy and balancing perspectives.* London: Hodder and Stoughton. pp 187-201.

Sciriha, C. (1990) The construction and use of a handwriting scale for Year 3 children. *Handwriting Review, 1990.* pp 12-16.

Stainthorp, R. and Hughes, D. (1995) (in press).

Weinberger, J (1993) Home as the primary context for young children's literacy development. In D. Wray (ed) *Literacy: Text and context.* Widnes: United Kingdom Reading Association. pp 167-175.

Wray, D., Bloom, W. and Hall, N. (1989) *Literacy in action.* London: The Falmer Press.

Ziviani, J. (1987) Pencil grasp and manipulation. In J. Alston and J. Taylor (eds) *Handwriting: Theory, research and practice.* Beckenham: Croom Helm. pp 24-46.

Evaluation of a Handwriting Assessment Procedure

Eve Blair
Institute for Child Health Research, Perth, W. Australia
Jenni Ballantyne
Second Skin, Perth, W. Australia
Sonya Horsman
The Cerebral Palsy Association, Coolbinia, W. Australia
Peter Chauvel
Princess Margaret Hospital for Children, Subiaco, W. Australia

INTRODUCTION

Primary school teachers continually assess the handwriting of their students using their experience. However, this is not considered sufficiently objective and reproducible when evaluating therapy. It has also been suggested that there may be advantages to applying more formal hand writing assessments even in the classroom (Hamstra-Bletz, 1994). We wished to evaluate the effect of a splinting technique on the handwriting of 13 self-selected primary school students aged 7 - 12 years with poor handwriting which had no obvious physical cause. We used an A-B single case experimental design (Barlow and Hersen, 1982) in which change in handwriting skills before and after a period without splint wear (period A) were compared with the change observed during a period of splint wear of equal duration (period B).

A search of the literature revealed various published handwriting assessments estimating absolute scores for handwriting enabling the comparison of individuals (Rubin and Henderson, 1982, Graham, 1986, Blandford and Lloyd, 1987 and Ziviani and Elkins, 1984). Since we wanted to measure change within the individual we devised a new test procedure based on those of published assessments.

This paper describes our test procedure, its intra- and inter- observer reliability and its validity in comparison with teacher and parents' perceptions.

The handwriting assessment procedure.

Eight attributes of writing ability were considered: one global attribute, legibility; 6 specific attributes, letter formation, consistency of letter size, spacing and of slant, alignment and line quality (thickness, smoothness, pressure) and speed. Speed was calculated by counting the number of letters written and dividing by the time taken. All other attributes were independently rated by 3 independent assessors from different professional disciplines. Since we wished to test whether the effect of the splints on writing were dependent on the cognitive input required at each assessment, 4 samples of text were requested, each by a different method. The first test entailed copying a short text hand written in the style currently taught in Western Australian primary schools. Cognitive input was minimised as style, spelling and content were all available. The second asked them to copy from a printed page, thereby requiring them to consider style. The third was a dictation with content provided, but style and spelling had to be considered and the last asked them to write a short memorised sentence followed by the alphabet, thereby requiring them to consider content as well as spelling and style. Since dictation speed is determined partially by the test administrator, the dictation of the first assessment was individually tape recorded for each subject and the recording played back at subsequent assessments. Thus speed did not vary between dictation samples. Speed was measured only for the other 3 samples. For each test the mean writing speed of the 2 pre-intervention samples was calculated and compared with writing speed of the post intervention samples.

Handwriting assessment scoring.

Three independent assessors were selected, one primary school teacher, one occupational therapist and one educational psychologist on the grounds that assessment may be dependent on the professional background of the assessor. No assessor was otherwise involved with the research nor was any previously acquainted with another assessor. The 3 assessors and 2 of the research team together discussed the writing attributes to be assessed and criteria for assessment were agreed upon. For each subject and for each of the 4 different tests the 3 samples were numbered in random order so that the assessors would be blind as to the temporal order of sample generation and to whether the splint was worn at the time of writing. The assessors then independently scored the samples labelled 2 and 3 relative to the sample labelled I using a value in the continuous range -2 to +2. Zero denoted that samples were of the same quality, deterioration was denoted by negative values and improvement by positive values. Thus samples were compared only within each subject. Change associated with splint wear for each subject, test and attribute was estimated by calculating the mean score over the first two assessments $S_m = (S_1-S_2)/2$ and subtracting S_m from the score of the third assessment (done while the splint was being worn after 8 weeks' splint exposure) S_3, giving S_3-S_m.

Assessors were asked to repeat the assessments on a sub-sample of the second test after a 3 week interval. For each assessor the intra class correlation (ICC) over the repeat, stratified by subject and attribute, estimated intra-rater reliability (Goldstein, 1987). Inter-assessor reliability was assessed by estimating ICCs over assessors using all samples stratified by subject, test and attribute.

Parent and teacher estimation of change in handwriting.

The validity of the formal handwriting assessments was gauged by comparing them with the opinions of teachers and parents concerning the effects of the splints on handwriting. These opinions were solicited by questionnaire at completion of the trial.

RESULTS

Intra-rater reliability

Intra class correlations (ICCs) across repeated scores by assessor and attribute are given in Table 1: higher ICC values denote greater reliability.

Intra-rater reliability varied between assessors and was consistently high across assessors for legibility. While higher ICCs were obtained by some assessors for other attributes (e.g. 0.95 for line quality by PT) it was not consistently high across all assessors. The highest mean ICC was attained by the assessor using the greatest range of scores (data not shown).

Table 1. Intra class correlations across repeated scores by assessor and attribute

Attribute	Assessor*			
	OT	EP	PT	Mean
Legibility	0.759	0.781	0.672	0.737
Letter formation	0.760	0.605	0.621	0.662
Consistency of:				
letter size	0.717	0.767	0.420	0.635
spacing	0.553	0.929	0.576	0.686
slope	0.496	0.803	0.513	0.604
Alignment	0.293	0.502	0.834	0.544
Line quality	0.532	0.831	0.951	0.771
Mean	0.587	0.745	0.655	

*OT = occupational therapist, EP = educational psychologist, PT = primary teacher

Inter-assessor reliability.

ICCs of scores across the 3 assessors are given by test and attribute in Table 2. The highest and most consistent ICCs across tests were attained for legibility and letter formation.

Classification of overall change in handwriting

If one attribute changed positively for a given subject, the change in other attributes also tended to be positive. In view of these observations, the effect of the splint on the handwriting quality of each subject was assigned a value in the range -2 to +2 after considering S_3-S_m values for all tests and giving more weight firstly to legibility and then to letter formation than to the other attributes.

Table 2. Intra class correlations of scores across 3 assessors by test and attribute.

Attribute	Copying Handwriting	Print	Writing from Memory	Dictation	Mean
Legibility	0.659	0.542	0.634	0.692	0.632
Letter formation	0.629	0.553	0.653	0.652	0.622
Consistency of					
letter size	0.586	0.308	0.344	0.297	0.384
spacing	0.417	0.556	0.546	0.345	0.466
slope	0.468	0.369	0.460	0.494	0.448
Alignment	0.457	0.513	0.416	0.686	0.518
Line quality	0.394	0.315	0.237	0.431	0.344
Mean	0.516	0.451	0.470	0.514	

Comparison of changes in speed with changes in other attributes.

Speed of writing increased in 6 subjects, changed little in 4 and 3 subjects wrote more slowly. Five of the 6 subjects who wrote faster showed no change in other writing attributes although the parents of 2 considered that their writing had improved. All 3 who wrote more slowly showed positive changes in other attributes. Thus changes in writing quality were inversely related to change in speed.

Comparison of formal, parental and teacher assessments of change in handwriting skills.

The parents of 13 and teachers of 10 subjects answered the questionnaire at completion of the trial. There was good agreement between teachers and parents as to which subjects had improved hand writing. In subjects whose teachers considered their handwriting to have improved after 8 weeks, improvements were reported in legibility (6/11) and willingness to write (7/11). No teacher reported changes in writing endurance, pencil grip or pressure on the paper. Increased speed and improved style were each reported by one teacher.

Since there was good agreement between parent and teacher assessments and because more parent than teacher data were available, the comparison of formal and parental assessments is shown in Table 3.

Table 3. A comparison of the parental assessment with the formal assessment of the effect of a splint on handwriting

Formal	Parental	Assessment	of the effect of	splint
	None	Positive	Very positive	Total
-1.5	0	1*	0	1
-.05	1	1*	1*	3
0	2	1*	0	3
+0.5	0	0	2*	2
+1	0	1	0	1
+2	0	1	2	3
Total	3	5	5	13

* Disagreement between parent and formal assessment

While there was broad agreement, parents reported positive effects for the 6 subjects starred in Table 3 for whom formal assessments were not or were only minimally positive. These subjects were examined individually.

1. The splint made marked improvements to the posture of the motor impaired subject who had the most negative S_3-S_m. He refused to wear his splint towards the end of the trial and obviously did not enjoy the formal assessments. We feel that the formal assessments may not have adequately measured his true capability particularly when he was wearing the splints.
2. The parents of the 5 other subjects with neutral or negative S_3-S_m and positive parental assessments perceived better writing endurance and/or a greater willingness to write, neither of which were considered in the formal assessments. Three of these 6 children were also formally assessed as writing faster, but since the 3 children whose parents reported that there had been no changes in hand writing also wrote faster, speed may not be considered important in the overall assessment of hand writing ability.

CONCLUSIONS

Intra- and inter- assessor reliability of scoring of this test was sufficiently high to enable pooling of results across assessors.

Legibility was the attribute most consistently reliable both within and between assessors. *A priori* legibility had been considered to be the attribute most important to perceived quality of handwriting and this is confirmed by the emphasis on legibility in the teachers' reports. In contrast speed was not considered an important aspect of writing ability in this group of subjects but factors that were not grounded in graphic skills, namely willingness to write and writing endurance were considered important. These were not addressed by the formal assessment but should be considered in future evaluations of therapy for handwriting.

The pattern of intra-assessor ICCs shown by attribute in Table 1 suggests that the importance attached to each attribute may vary with the discipline of the assessor. For example, alignment may be considered of less importance by occupational therapists and educational psychologists than by school teachers, but because of our small sample, this should be confirmed in other data sets.

As anticipated, given that ICCs compare variability of score with score value, the assessor with greatest reliability (EP) used the greatest range of scores. Reliability may therefore be increased by allowing a greater range of scores, e.g. using a range of -5 to +5 rather than -2 to +2.

We conclude that the test is a valid measure of graphic skills provided the subject is willing to perform under the test conditions, but does not address other important aspects of writing ability.

Acknowlegements

We would like to thank the Public Endowment Trust of Western Australia for financial assistance and all the subjects and their parents who gave up their Sunday mornings to attend assessments.

References

Barlow, D. H. & Hersen, M. (1984). A-B design. Section 5.2 in *Single case experimental designs: strategies for studying behaviour change*. Sydney: Pergamon Press. pp. 142-152.

Blandford, B. J. & Lloyd, J. W. (1987) Effects of a self-instructional procedure on handwriting. *Journal of Learning Disabilities*, **20**, 342-346.

Goldstein, H. (1987) *Multilevel modelling in educational and social research*. Charles Griffin & Company Ltd. p. 13.

Graham, S. (1986) The reliability, validity and utility of three handwriting measurement procedures. *Journal of Educational Research*, **79**, 373-380.

Hamstra-Bletz, L. (1994). The teacher as a judge of handwriting quality. *Handwriting Review 1994*. 12- 14

Rubin, N. & Henderson, S. E. (1982) Two sides of the same coin: variations in teaching methods and failure to learn to write. *Special Education Forward Trends*, **9**, 17-24.

Ziviani, J. & Elkins, J. 1984. An evaluation of handwriting performance. *Educational Review*, **36**, 249-261.

A Case Study of Developmental Motor Dysgraphia

Deborah Dewey
Department of Paediatrics,University of Calgary, Canada
David Roeltgen
Williamsport Hospital, Williamsport, PA

The idea that developmental dysgraphia is a unitary syndrome has been superseded by the documentation of a number of distinct subtypes of dysgraphia (Denckla & Roeltgen, 1992; Sandler, Watson, Footo, Levine, Coleman, & Hooper, 1992). Most recent analyses of acquired agraphia distinguish between disorders of "spelling" (i.e., linguistic agraphias) and disorders of "writing" (i.e., apraxic agraphias) (Baxter, & Warrington, 1986; Roeltgen & Heilman, 1985). When applying these analyses to developmental disorders, "spelling" dysgraphias should have a disturbance in letter or word choice, but the actual written form of the letters should remain intact. Further, children with "spelling" dysgraphias should demonstrate little or no difference between oral and written spelling skills (Roeltgen, 1992). In contrast, children with "writing" dysgraphias or apraxic dysgraphias should not have a problem with letter or word choice but rather with poor letter formation. Further, the "writing" deficit demonstrated by these children should not be explained by peripheral weakness or clumsiness, sensory problems, confusion or impaired reasoning (Denckla & Roeltgen, 1992).

Rothi and Heilman (1981) proposed that there is a graphemic area that is responsible for distinguishing the individual features of a grapheme. This function would be necessary for successful letter reading and successful recognition of correctly formed graphemes. They also propose that it is responsible for programming movements used in writing. They postulated that this system was the one that was disrupted in patients with acquired apraxic agraphia. Studies that have investigated apraxic agraphia in patients with acquired brain lesions have reported that this disorder is characterised by poorly formed or illegible spontaneous writing and illegible writing to dictation with an improvement in writing with copying and intact oral spelling ability (Valenstein & Heilman, 1979; Roeltgen & Heilman, 1985), and is dissociable from disordered reading. Although most patients with apraxic agraphia have a limb apraxia (Denckla & Roeltgen, 1992), some patients have been described as demonstrating apraxic agraphia without apraxia (Baxter & Warrington, 1986; Croisile, Laurent, Michel, & Trillet, 1990; Margolin & Binder, 1984; Roeltgen & Heilman, 1983). These studies have reported that the writing skills of these patients resemble those of patients with apraxic agraphia and apraxia.

Another motor agraphia that has been reported in adults is agraphia secondary to impairment of the allographic system (Black, Bass, Behrmann, & Hacker, 1987; DeBastiani & Barry, 1989; Yopp & Roeltgen, 1987). Patients with this impairment have the ability to write under most conditions but make errors of case. The disturbance frequently involves substituting the incorrect case. A disturbance of the allographic system in children might present differently. As a developmental disorder, impairment of the allographic system should lead to poor formation of letters and more prominent agraphia when writing in a particular case.

The identification of "pure" cases of disturbed motor (i.e., apraxic) agraphia requires that the disturbed writing occurs in the absence of disturbed oral spelling, reading and language, as well as, disturbed praxis and visual-perceptual skills. In the developmental setting, a generalised agraphic impairment of the ideational type would produce poor hand writing that would improve with slavish copying. Impairment of the allographic system should lead to poorer writing when one particular case is used.

Few reports of children with developmental dysgraphia that fit the criteria for "pure" motor agraphia have been published (but see Denckla & Roeltgen, 1992; Rapin, Mattis, Rowan, & Golden, 1977), and none of these has been systematically studied to determine if all criteria for this diagnosis have been fulfilled. However, the following systematic investigation describes a child with a disturbance in printing that is especially marked when printing upper case letters. One task that emphasised slavish copying was performed relatively well. Further, this disturbance in printing occurred in the absence of any impairments in intellectual, memory, language, oral spelling, praxis, visual-motor, visual-perceptual or fine motor abilities. Thus, this child fulfils the requirements of pure motor dysgraphia best characterised as ideational apraxic dysgraphia with selective involvement of that aspect of the allographic systemused in the production of upper case letters.

METHOD

Case Report

At the time of testing P.F. was an 8 year 4 month old boy in the second grade. Past medical history reveals that he was born at 26 weeks gestation by caesarean section and weighed 1020 grams. The pregnancy had been complicated by repeated antipartum haemorrhage. His Apgar scores were 5 and 6 at one and 5 minutes, respectively. He had transient tachypnea requiring ventilation for only 2 days. His perinatal course was complicated by bradycardia and recurrent apnea. Following his birth P.F. was in the hospital for a total of 97 days.

P.F. was seen at the Perinatal Follow-up Clinic at Alberta Children's Hospital at ages 4, 8, 11, 18 and 36 months (these ages were adjusted for prematurity). Assessments of various developmental skills were completed at these ages. P.F.'s cognitive skills were assessed at ages 8 months adjusted age and 18 months adjusted age using the Bayley Scales of Infant Development. At both of these times, P.F. was found to be functioning above the average for his adjusted age. At 36 months adjusted age, P.F.'s cognitive skills were assessed using the Stanford Binet Intelligence Scale-Fourth Edition and were found to be in the high average range. He showed strong verbal reasoning abilities and had above average short-term memory skills. Number concepts and visual pattern analysis were also considered to be above average.

Assessments of speech and language, hearing, and motor skills were also completed by the Perinatal Follow-up Clinic. Results indicated that P.F. had normal hearing and normal eardrum motility. Speech and language assessments completed when P.F. was 11 months adjusted age, 18 months adjusted age and 36 months adjusted age indicated that he was functioning in the normal range for development of receptive and expressive language skills. Assessment of gross motor skills at 36 months adjusted age indicated that muscle tone was normal and that gross motor functioning was within the normal range for his age.

At age 4 years P.F. suffered a head injury. No loss of consciousness was reported, however, his mother stated that he was confused and disoriented until the following day. His mother also reported that he experienced headaches on and off for two weeks following the head injury. Other difficulties noted by P.F.'s mother after the head injury were phrase reversals, clumsiness, and increased short temper. Neurological examination of basic motor functions and language skills 2 months after this injury did not find that P.F. demonstrated significant problems in these areas. No phrase reversals or clumsiness were noted during the examination. Thus, it was concluded that the phrase reversals and clumsiness noted by P.F.'s mother were due to a mild post concussive syndrome and that there was no evidence of serious brain injury.

When P.F. was 5 years 6 months of age, he was referred to the Neurology Clinic at Alberta Children's Hospital because of parental concerns regarding word reversals and clumsiness. Radiological exam at this time indicated that there was no evidence of an old or recent skull fracture and no suggestion of raised intracranial pressure. P.F. produced no word reversals on speech and language assessment. Further, it indicated that P.F.'s ability to use and understand language was in the average range for his age. An occupational therapy assessment indicated that visual-perceptual, visual-motor, fine motor and gross motor skills were in the average range. Thus, assessment of motor skills before (i.e., 36 months) and after (i.e., 5 years 6 months) the head injury revealed that P.F. demonstrated normal motor function.

Education history reveals that P.F. had been retained in grade 2 because of his extreme difficulty with writing skills. According to parental report, P.F. does not demonstrate any other academic difficulties.

Psychological Test Findings

P.F.'s test scores are summarised in Table 1. On the Wechsler Intelligence Scale for Children-Third Edition (WISC-III; Wechsler, 1991), P.F. scored in the average range in tests of verbal skills and nonverbal skills. All of the subtest scores fell within the average range with the exception of his above average scores on Information and Picture Completion. His speech was fluent and well articulated. Assessment of his understanding of language as measured by the Peabody Picture Vocabulary Test - Revised (PPVT-R; Dunn & Dunn, 1981) was found to be in the high average range. His performance on the on the Clinical Evaluation of Language Fundamentals-Revised Screening Test (CELF-R; Semel, Wiig, & Secord, 1989), a test which assesses more complex language functions such as sentence construction and verbal problem solving, indicated that he was functioning significantly above criterion for his age. Assessment of visual and verbal memory skills with the Wide Range Assessment of Memory and Learning (WRAML; Sheslow & Adams, 1990) indicated that P.F.'s memory skills

Table 1. P.F.'s Psychological Test Scores

Psychological Test	Standard Score	Percentile
Wisc-111		
Verbal IQ	110	75
Information	14	
Similiarities	13	
Arithmetic	8	
Vocabulary	13	
Comprehension	10	
Performance IQ	106	66
Picture Completion	14	
Coding	11	
Picture Arrangement	8	
Block Design	13	
Object Assembly	8	
Full Scale IQ	108	70
Language		
PPVT-R	114	82
CELF-R Screening (raw score)	38	criterion score for age is 24
Memory		
WRAML Verbal Memory Index	128	97
WRAML Visual Memory Index	107	68
WRAMLLearning Index	128	97
WRAMLGeneral Memory Index	127	96
Visual-Motor Abilities		
VMI	102	55
Visual-Perceptual Abilities		
TVPS	135	99
Fine Motor		
BOTMP-Fine Motor Composite	51	54
Academic Achievment		
WJ-R Broad Reading	108	69
WJR- Mathematics	92	29
WJ-R Broad Written Language	74	4
WRAT-R Spelling (Oral)	94	34
WRAT-R Spelling (Written)	81	10

were above average. Visual-motor skills were assessed using the Developmental Tests of Visual Motor Integration (VMI; Beery, 1989). On this measure P.F. achieved a scaled score of 102 (55th percentile).

Assessment of visual-perceptual skills with the Tests of Visual Perceptual Skills (TVPS; Gardner, 1988) indicated that these skills were intact. The Bruininks-Oseretsky Test of Motor Proficiency Fine Motor Composite (BOTMP; Bruininks, 1978) revealed that P.F.'s fine motor skills were in the average range (54th percentile).

Reading, mathematics, and writing skills assessed using the Woodcock-Johnson Psychoeducational Battery-Revised (WJ-R; Woodcock & Johnson, 1989) indicated that reading and mathematics skills were at age level, while written language skills were significantly delayed. Specifically, P.F. demonstrated significant delays on tasks that demanded knowledge of letter form, spelling, punctuation, capitalisation, production of single word responses to pictures and the production of sentences to pictures. P.F.'s ability to spell words orally was found to be in the average range, however, his ability to print these same words to dictation was found to be in the low average range (i.e., Wide Range Achievement Test-Revised; WRAT-R; Jastak & Wilkinson, 1984).

Praxis skills were assessed with a representational gestures test. The representational gestures test which was similar to that used by Dewey and Kaplan (1992) and Raade, Rothi and Heilman (1991), involved performing six transitive limb gestures and six intransitive limb gestures to command and imitation (see Appendix 1). During testing P.F.'s performance was videotaped by a camera placed approximately 6 feet from him. The camera was focused on his upper body, including the upper limb and facial area. P.F. was instructed to perform the gestures as carefully and accurately as possible. An error analysis similar to that used in Dewey (1993) was used to assess gestural performance. This error classification system consisted of 8 major categories: correct gestures, delay in initiating movement, added movements, movement errors, posture errors, action errors, location errors. Scoring was done by two independent raters using the videotapes of P.F.'s performance. Examination of the errors made by P.F. indicated that the majority of errors were location errors, specifically, errors of extent (i.e., extent of the object not taken into account when demonstrating object use). He also demonstrated some postural errors (i.e., incorrect position or shape of the limb structure), however, no body-part-as-object errors were noted. According to Kaplan (1968, 1977), errors of extent were the predominant gestural error demonstrated by normally developing children at age 8. Body-part-as-object errors decreased to less than 25 percent frequency among normally developing 8 year old children. Thus, the types of praxis errors demonstrated by P.F. when performing gestures appear to be consistent with what one would expect of a child his age suggesting that praxis development was normal.

During the assessment session, P.F. was observed to use his right hand for printing and other motor tasks such as cutting out a circle with a scissors and moving pegs. Examination of some of P.F.'s school work indicated that he had appeared to have less difficulty copying letters and words, than producing legible printing when spontaneously printing or when printing to dictation.

Experimental Tests

P.F. was first asked to compare samples of printing that consisted of 6 to 8 word sentences and identify which was better (i.e., neater). On all 10 trials, P.F. correctly identified the printing that was "neater", indicating that he was aware of what was considered "good" printing and what was not.

Eleven experimental handwriting tasks were used to further assess P.F.'s writing problems. These included spontaneous printing of the alphabet first in lower case and then in upper case letters, printing of a spontaneous sentence in response to a picture, printing of a spontaneous paragraph in response to a picture, direct copying (with the stimulus immediately above or beside the line of response) of letters and sentences, printing sentences to dictation, transposing sentences printed in upper case to lower case, transposing sentences printed in lower case to upper case, and a "slavish copy" task that required copying letters of increasing size within lines of increasing width.

All of the handwriting tasks were scored by two independent raters utilising a system modified after Freeman (1915) and used previously in studying developmental dysgraphia (Denckla & Roeltgen, 1992; Roeltgen, 1989). The raters were blinded to the child's diagnosis and the goals of the study. This system assessed five areas important to handwriting quality: consistency of slant, consistency of height, quality of line drawn, consistency of spacing between letters, frequency of letters off of the line and letter form. All of the items except letter form were scored from one to five (one being the lowest, five being the highest) and letter form was scored from one to ten, thus giving letter form double weighting. In comparing the scoring of each item by the two raters who were experienced in this method of scoring handwriting, there was an 89.1% agreement. Agreement was defined as scores by one of the raters within one point (on the 1-5 scale) of the other rater. The exception to this was letter form where a range of two points (on the 1-10 scale) was accepted as agreement. The mean scores of the raters for the handwriting tasks are presented in Table 2.

Table 2. Performance on the Printing Tasks

Task	P.F. Mean score	NormalChildren Mean score	Range
Alphabet in lower case letters	21.0		
Alphabet in upper case letters	15.5		
Direct copy of letters	18.5		
"Slavish copy" of letters	20.0		
Direct copy of sentences	15.5	26.3	18 - 34
Sentences to dictation	17.0	25.1	19 - 31
Spontaneous sentence in response to picture	18.5	24.1	13 - 33
Spontaneous paragraph in response to picture	16.5		
Transpose lower case to upper case	13.5		
Transpose upper case to lower case	14.5		

Note: Maximum mean score on the printing task was 35. The scores for the normal children are based on data from children aged 7 to 10 years of age.

Examination of P.F.'s spontaneous printing of the letters of the alphabet first in lower case and then in upper case letters indicated that with both cases he had problems with case size (see Figure 1). This was particularly marked, however, on the task requiring the production of upper case letters. It was also noted that with both lower and upper case letters P.F. had problems with reversals, and letter formation/substitutions (i.e., h for n, Y for U) . In addition, he missed printing some letters in the lower case alphabet (i.e., c, k) and missequenced some letters in the upper case alphabet (i.e., J, K, J, L). In contrast, P.F.'s copies of both upper and lower case letters were accurate in terms of case size and he did not demonstrate any reversal (see Figure 1). Also, P.F. displayed surprisingly good performance on a "slavish copying" task that required him to copy lower and upper case letters of increasing size within lines of increasing width (see Figure 2). Again, he did not demonstrate any problems in terms of case size or reversals.

P.F.'s ability to copy sentences, to print sentences to dictation, to print a sentence and a paragraph spontaneously in response to a picture was also

Figure 1. Examples of printing and copying of letters (1) lower case alphabet printed spontaneously, (2) uppercase alphabet printed spontaneously, and (3) direct copy of lower case and upper case letters.

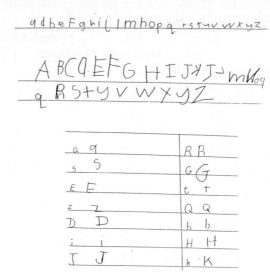

Figure 2. Examples of "slavish copy" of lower case and upper case letters.

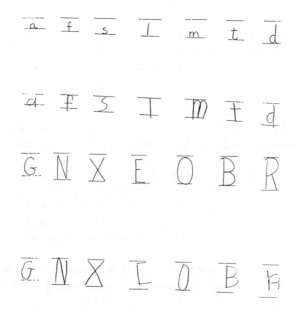

Figure 3. Examples of (1) direct copying of a sentence, (2) printing a sentence to dictation, and (3) printing a sentence spontaneously in response to a picture.

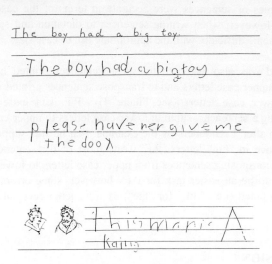

Figure 4. Examples of transposing sentences (1) from lower case to upper case, and (2) from upper case to lower case.

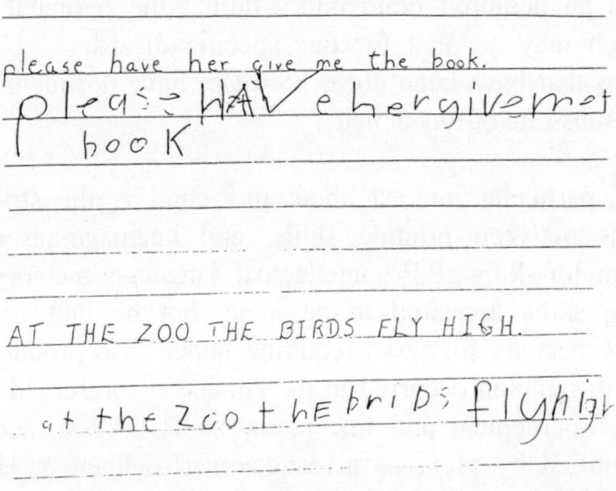

assessed. Examination of his performance indicated that he had difficulty with all of these printing tasks (see Figure 3). Overall his performance on each of these printing tasks was similar. Of note, however is that P.F.'s direct copies of sentences were accurate in terms of the case size of the letters. However, when writing sentences to dictation and spontaneously, P.F. had some difficulty with the appropriate use of case size

This child was also asked to transpose sentences printed in lower case letters to upper case letters and to transpose sentences printed in upper case letters lower case letters (see Figure 4). P.F. had extreme difficulty transposing a sentence written in lower case letters to upper case letters. In fact, even after 2 reminders by the examiner that he was supposed to write the sentence in "big" letters, P.F. wrote most of the sentence in "small" letters. Transposing sentences from upper case letters to lower case letters appeared to be an easier task for P.F., however, some errors in case size were still noted (i.e., "thE" for "the") as were letter reversals ("birbs" for "birds").

DISCUSSION

Whether P.F. demonstrates an "acquired" versus a "developmental" disorder is a question which cannot be answered on the basis of the present evidence. P.F.'s developmental history suggests that he may have experienced an acquired brain injury during the perinatal or pre-school period which may account for this specific disorder. The radiological examinations that have been done, however, have not identified a specific anatomical substrate of this deficit.

What is of particular interest about this child is the striking cognitive dissociations between printing skills, and language-based and visual-perceptual-motor skills. P.F.'s intellectual, language, memory, oral spelling and reading skills appeared to be intact but he had very poor letter production especially for tasks requiring upper case production. Further, this severe dysgraphia occurred in the context of preserved praxis, visual-motor, visual-perceptual and fine motor skills. Thus, according to the criteria identified by previous investigators (Roeltgen & Heilman, 1985; Valenstein & Heilman, 1979), P.F. displays a motor or apraxic agraphia. P.F. demonstrated good praxis and an improvement in printing on the "slavish copying" task relative to most of the other printing tasks. This suggests that this disorder is best termed, based on analogy with acquired dyspraxia in adults ideational apraxic dysgraphia. According to Baxter and

Warrington (1986), patients with ideational agraphia have no apraxia but have poor handwriting that improved with copying.

P.F.'s scores on only two of the handwriting tasks approached the scores that would be expected of a child his age. These are slavish copying of letters and producing the alphabet in lower case letters. The first result is typical of what would be expected in ideational apraxic dysgraphia. The second result would not be predicted based on what is known about acquired ideational apraxic agraphia. Spontaneously writing the alphabet is for children a well-practised, probably overlearned, and to some extent, automatic production. In acquired language disorders, perseverations of more overlearned, automatic productions is common. In addition, the concepts developed from acquired disorders, though useful, rarely map directly onto developmental disorders (Roeltgen & Blaskey, 1992). Influences such as education and the differences between a lesion in a developing brain rather than a relatively stable brain cannot be under emphasized. Therefore, although ideational apraxia dysgraphia appears to be an appropriate diagnostic term for the dysgraphia produced by this child, further studies of childhood dysgraphia are needed to determine the generalizability of this concept and the consistency of all of its features.

P.F.'s poor performance on most tasks requiring upper case letters suggests that there was also a disturbance of the allographic system which is important for directing the handwriting systems in the production of the correct case (upper or lower) and style (cursive or print). This to is an area of investigation relatively unexplored in childhood dysgraphia. Many questions regarding frequency, consistency of features and mechanisms remain to be answered.

In summary, this subject was found to have a selective impairment in his ability to print, especially for tasks requiring upper case production, despite having no difficulty accessing the correct motor programs for other learned motor activities. His primary difficulty appeared to be not in the execution of the letter form but at the level of access to the appropriate motor programmes or sequences necessary for producing letters, especially upper case letters.

Rothi and Heilman (1981) proposed that there was a graphemic area which was necessary for guiding the motor programming in grapheme production. Further, they postulated that this was the system that was disrupted in patients with acquired apraxic agraphia. More recently, Denckla and Roeltgen (1992) have described a cognitive developmental model of handwriting that incorporates Rothi and Heilman's proposed "graphemic area" (i.e., graphemic system; see Figure 5). According to this model, there are many cognitive systems which can impact on the production of normal handwriting and its development in children. Examination of P.F.'s difficulties with printing within the context of this model suggests that his difficulties with printing are due to disturbances in both the graphemic system and the allographic store. P.F.'s good oral spelling relative to his printed spelling, good visual-motor, perceptual-motor and fine motor skills and his poor performance on tasks requiring upper case letters support this conclusion. Also, the fact that P.F. did not demonstrate deficits in praxis suggests that the impairment of the graphemic system can be selective and not associated with a more generalised developmental dyspraxia (Denckla and Roeltgen, 1992). These findings provide support for the idea that dysfunction of the graphemic system and the allographic store could account for children such as P.F. who demonstrate poor handwriting, normal intellectual, language and memory skills, normal visual-motor and visual-perceptual abilities, normal praxis, and normal fine motor function.

Figure 5 A cognitive developmental model of handwriting. Denckla and Roeltgen (1992)

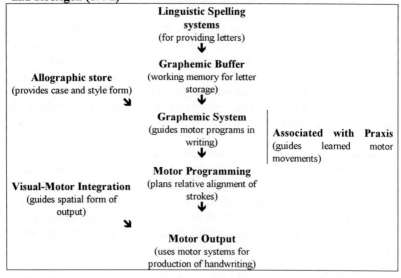

Regarding the treatment of writing disorders in children, we feel that it is a mistake to assume that by giving a child with motor dysgraphia more practice with writing that writing skills will improve. Instead, before any type of appropriate remediation plan can be developed, it is important to complete a careful assessment of the child's writing problems. Such an assessment may provide one with some indication as to the nature of the underlying processes or mechanisms which may be contributing to the child's writing difficulties. The cognitive model of handwriting proposed by Denckla and Roeltgen (1992) suggests that there are at least six cognitive systems (i.e., graphemic buffer, graphemic system, allographic store, praxis, motor planning, visual motor integration) that may be responsible for poor handwriting in children who demonstrate motor dysgraphias. Further, this model does not attempt to account for the many different types of linguistic problems that may be associated with poor handwriting in children. Thus, before appropriate remediation programs for children with writing problems can be developed research is needed that investigates the cognitive components that are necessary for the development of writing skills and that systematically assesses the components which breakdown in children with developmental dysgraphia.

Authors' Notes

Support for this study was provided by the grants from the University of Calgary and the Alberta Children's Hospital foundation. We would like to thank P.F. and his mother for their cooperation and assistance.

References

Baxter, D. M., & Warrington, E. K. (1986). Ideational agraphia: A single case study. *Journal of Neurology, Neurosurgery. & Psychiatry*, **49**, 369-374.

Beery, K. E. (1989). *Developmental Test of Visual Motor Integration*. Cleveland, OH: Modern Curriculum Press.

Black, S. E., Bass, K., Behrmann, M., & Hacker, P. (1987). Selective writing impairment: A single case study of a deficit in allographic conversion. *Neurology*, **37**, 174.

Bruininks, R.H. (1978). *Bruininks-Oseretsky Test of Motor Proficiency*. Circle Pines .MN: American Guidance Services.

Croisile, L., Laurent, B., Michel, D., & Trillet, M. (1990). Pure agraphia after deep left hemisphere haematoma. *Journal of Neurology, Neurosurgery and Psychiatry*, **53**, 263-265.

DeBastiani, K. & Barry, C. (1989). A cognitive analysis of an acquired dysgraphia patient with 'allographic' writing disorder. *Cognitive Neuropsychology*, **6**, 25-41.

Denckla, M. B., & Roeltgen, D. P. (1992). Disorders of motor function and control. In I. Rapin & S.J. Segalowitz (Eds.), *Handbook of neuropsychology, Vol. 6. Child neuropsychology* (pp.455-476). Amsterdam: Elsevier.

Dewey, D. (1993). Error analysis of limb and orofacial praxis in children withdevelopmental motor deficits. *Brain and Cognition*, 23, 203-221.

Dewey, D. & Kaplan, B.J. (1992). Analysis of praxis task demands in the assessment of children with developmental motor deficits. *Developmental Neuropsychology*, **8**, 367-379.

Dunn, L. M. & Dunn, L. M. (1981). *Peabody Picture Vocabulary Test - Revised.* Circle Pines, MN: American Guidance Services.

Freeman, F. N. (1915). An analytical scale for judging handwriting. *Elementary School Journal*, 432-441.

Gardner, M. F. (1989). *Test of Visual-Perceptual Skills.* San Francisco, CA: Health Publishing Co.

Jastak, S., & Wilkinson, g.S. (1984). *Wide Range Achievement Test-Revised.* Wilmington, DE: Jastak Associates.

Margolin, D. I., & Binder, L. (1984). Multiple component agraphia in a patient with atypical cerebral dominance: An error analysis. *Brain and Language*, **22**, 26-40.

Raade, A. S., Rothi, L. J., & Heilman, K. M. (1991). The relationship between buccofacial and limb apraxia. *Brain and Cognition*, **16**, 130-146.

Rapin, I., Mattis, S., Rowan, A. J., & Golden, G. C. (1977). Verbal auditory agnosia in children. *Developmental Medicine and Child Neurology,* **19**, 192-207.

Roeltgen, D. P. (1989). Prospective analysis of a model of writing, anatomic aspects. Presented at the Academy of Aphasia, Santa Fe, NM.

Roeltgen, D.P. (1992) Phonological error analysis development and empirical evaluation. *Brain and Language*, **43**, 190-229.

Roeltgen, D.P. & Blaskey P. (1992). Processes, breakdowns and remediation in developmental disorders of reading and spelling. In D. I. Margolin (ed.), *Cognitive neuropsycholoqy in clinical practice* (pp. 298-326). New York: Oxford University Press.

Roeltgen, D. P., & Heilman, K. M. (1983). Apractic agraphia in a patient with normal praxis. *Brain and Language*, **18**, 811-827.

Roeltgen, D. P., & Heilman, K. M. (1985). Review of agraphia and proposal for an anatomically-based neuropsychological model of writing. *Applied Psycholinguistics*, **6**, 205-230.

Rothi, L. J., & Heilman, K. M., (1981). Alexia and agraphia with spared spelling and letter recognition abilities. *Brain and Language*, **12**, 1-13.

Sandler, M. D., Watson, F. E., Footo, M., Levine, M. D., Coleman, W. L., & Hooper, S. R. (1992). Neurodevelopmental study of writing disorders in middle childhood. *Journal of Developmental and Behavioural Pediatrics,* **13**, 17-23.

Semel, E., Wiig, E. H., Secord, W. (1989). *Clinical Evaluation of Language Fundamentals-Revised Screening Test.* New York: The Psychological Corporation.

Sheslow, D. & Adams, W. (1990). *Wide Range Assessment of Memory and Learning.* Wilmington, DE: Jastak Associates.

Valenstein, E. & Heilman, K. M. (1979). Apraxic agraphia with neglect-induced paragraphia. *Archives of Neurology,* **67**, 44-56.

Wechsler (1991). *Wechsler Intelligence Scale for Children-Third Edition.* New York: The Psychological Corporation.

Woodcock, R. W. & Johnson, M. B. (1989). *Woodcock Johnson Psychoeducational Battery-Revised.* Allen, TX: DLM Teaching Resources.

Yopp, K. S., & Roeltgen, D. P. (1987). Case of alexia and agraphia due to a disconnection of the visual input to and the motor output from an intact graphemic area. *Journal of Clinical and Experimental Neuropsychology,* **9**. 42.

Appendix 1: List of Limb Gestures Used in the Praxis Test

Limb Transitive
1. Show me how you brush your teeth with a tooth brush.
2. Show me how you comb your hair with a comb.
3. Show me how you eat ice cream with a spoon.
4. Show me how youhit a nail with a hammer.
5. Show me how you cut paper with scissors.
6. Show me how you print your name with a pencil.

Limb Intransitive
1. Show me how you salute.
2. Show me how you snap your fingers.
3. Show me how you wave goodbye.
4. Show me how youcross your fingers.
5. Show me how you make a fist.
6. Show me how you pinch your nose.

Vision for Writing

Keith Holland
Optometrist, Cheltenham

Although handwriting is receiving increasing attention, both within the educational professions, and in the media, it seems that relatively little attention is being paid to the mechanics of writing, and in particular to the preparedness of the pupil to engage in what is probably the most complex motor task the human is capable of undertaking. This contribution is aimed at alerting all those working with handwriting to the need for good visual abilities as a pre-requisite for optimum writing efficiency.

The effect of vision on handwriting can easily be demonstrated - simply close the eyes whilst you are writing! What is not immediately apparent however, is the contribution of poorly developed, or skewed visual skills on the fine-motor co-ordination skills of an individual. Appreciation of these skills, and of the signs and symptoms that typically indicate visual difficulties should assist teachers in identifying those individuals at risk, and in arranging prompt referral for visual investigation. Much of the work in this field is not recent - indeed as long ago as 1958, researchers were advocating the need for appropriately sloped writing surfaces.

What are the main visual skills for writing? There are probably three main physical skills that underpin all other areas of visual perception. As Optometrists we are interested not only in the skills in isolation, but in the relationship between skills, and the effective integration of all aspects of visual functioning at near. Consider figure one. This is a sample of writing from a child at the initial visual examination. Although the child could "see" well, and passed conventional eye tests, it was found that there was difficulty in integrating the necessary visual skills at near. When these problems were attended to, by means of spectacles and some simple vision therapy, the result was the writing seen in figure two. This represented a time interval of some three weeks from the sample in figure one, yet the improvement in quality could represent some two years of maturity in conventional terms.

Figure 1. The handwriting of a ten year old prior to Optometric Intervention.

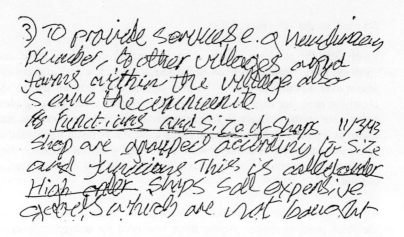

Figure 2. The Handwriting of the same ten year old after Optometric help.

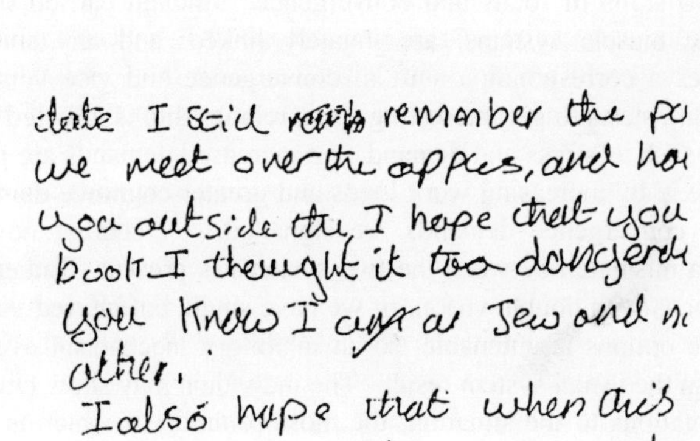

This child still obviously required attention to the *mechanics* of writing, and perhaps a course of structured writing instruction, but the primary afferent difficulties had at least been dealt with.

So what are the key visual skills?

Firstly, can the child see clearly at an appropriate working distance, and (perhaps more importantly) can he or she sustain clear and comfortable vision over a period of time. The long-sighted child may be able to see clearly at near, but only by exerting excessive effort in maintaining clear focus. He or she is likely to fatigue prematurely, and concentration may suffer as a result. A breakdown in focus control may result in blurring of print, but many children simply look away briefly before renewing their efforts at near, readily being distracted, and showing poor concentration as a result.

The second skills area to consider is -- the ability to direct the two eyes to the same point in space. Again, there is a need for convergence to be sustainable; premature fatiguing of the system can lead to concentration loss and distractibility.

The two skills of focus and convergence, although carried out by quite separate muscle systems, are innately linked, and any shift in focus produces a corresponding shift in convergence and vice versa. This is where life starts to get interesting - this relationship is affected by external factors such as stress and demand. As increased demands are placed upon focus (e.g. by increasing work loads and greater cognitive demands), then greater convergence demands are signalled. A conflict now arises in which a mismatch between the two systems is present. Either we obtain clear focus with double vision, or we have single but blurred vision Either of these options is untenable, so an inhibitory mechanism overrides, and skews in the visual system result. The individual may show one of a range of adaptations to the situation, the most common of which is probably a reduction in working distance.

The most efficient distance for visual control is generally regarded as the Harmon distance - the distance from the elbow joint to the middle knuckle This distance was postulated following extensive myographic studies on visual stress and working distance, carried out over thirty years ago. To date this work has not been superseded. A reduction in working distance from this has been shown to lead to increased muscle tension, and lowered efficiency - often affecting writing.

So-called "Near Point Stress" has been recognised for many years as a factor in reduced visuo-motor performance, but there would appear to have been little cross-talk between Optometry and Education about the signs, symptoms and treatment for this problem, which reports suggest may affect some thirty five percent of all school children.

The third main skills area is that of eye movement (sometimes erroneously called tracking). The ability to sequence eye movements in an orderly and controlled left to right manner is essential for good reading, and for good handwriting. Weakness' in these skills often lead to reduced perceptual performances, increased letter reversals, problems with letter ordering, and can subsequently affect the development of good visualisation skills-- essential for non-phonetic spelling.

So what are the typical signs of a child with a visual difficulty? Figure 3 shows a typical questionnaire that can be used by teachers and psychologists to identify children at risk. This should provide information to encourage parents to take their children for more detailed visual assessments, preferably with an Optometrist who has a particular interest in vision-related learning difficulties, or with a Behavioural Optometrist. The information on checklists such as this can be of great value to the optometrist and a copy should always be given to the parents to pass on. The routine school eye test does not normally include any tests of near visual performance, and cannot be relied upon to give any indication of potential problems.

It should also be noted that children with writing difficulties often (but by no means always) have some problems with reading, and attention to the visual problems can produce remarkable changes in reading fluency and accuracy.

The Optometrist may prescribe lenses for use at near, and may also start the child on a programme of vision therapy activities. These will be designed to improve visual-motor co-ordination through a series of experiential tasks that challenge vision development, and lead to the development of improved visual skills (ref 4 here). In particular, the ability accurately to co-ordinate hand, finger and arm movements with visual directions in an effortless and sustainable fashion is vital. The use of lenses to correct skews in visual performance has been the subject of a great deal of research over the last twenty years or more, yet still seems to be a little known area in the UK, where most spectacles are prescribed

Figure 3. A teachers' checklist of visual difficulties
Confidential
TEACHERS' CHECKLIST FOR VISUAL SIGNS
Child's Name.. Form/Teacher/Reference........
1 *Please circle the special areas (if any) of difficulty this child has.*

Vocabulary   Word Recognition   Oral reading   Silent Reading   Rate   Interpretation
Attention   Comprehension   Handwriting   Spelling

2 *Four classifications of frequency of performance traits are given:*

A - Meaning very often observed (many times a day)
B - Meaning regularly observed (daily)
C - Meaning sometimes observed
D - Meaning seldom observed

Please ring the letter you best consider indicates the child's performance

Does the child show any of the following?

a	Skipping or rereading lines or words	A	B	C	D
b	Reads too slowly	A	B	C	D
c	Uses finger or marker as pointer when reading	A	B	C	D
d	Lacks ability to remember what s/he has read	A	B	C	D
e	Shows fatigue or listlessness when reading	A	B	C	D
f	Complains of print "running together" or "jumping"	A	B	C	D
g	Gets too close to reading and writing tasks	A	B	C	D
h	Loss of attention to task at hand	A	B	C	D
i	Distracted by other activities	A	B	C	D
j	Assumes an improper or awkward sitting posture	A	B	C	D
k	Writes crookedly, poorly spaced letters, cannot stay on ruled lines, excessive pressure used	A	B	C	D
l	Orients drawings poorly on paper	A	B	C	D
m	Is seen to blink frequently	A	B	C	D
n	Rubs eyes excessively	A	B	C	D

General observations

o	Clumsiness and difficulty manipulating own body and other objects in space available, including problems with ball control	A	B	C	D
p	Awareness of things around him in the classroom to point where s/he turns to look at stimulus	A	B	C	D
q	Is this child able to maintain involvement with your instruction?	A	B	C	D

Scoring

Any scores of 'A', more than two scores of 'B', and more than 3 or 4 scores of 'C' suggests that prompt referral to an Optometrist specialising in children's eye care is indicated. A copy of this check list would also be helpful to the Optometrist.

simply for the correction of refractive error at distance, with little or no account being taken as to the effect at the near-point.

So, what can teachers and educators do?

The first, and most vital contribution the teacher can make is to identify the child who is having visual difficulties. Use of the chart (figure 3) can be helpful here. It is NOT sufficient to rely on school visual screenings, since no tests of near-point difficulties are carried out. Should visual problems be suspected, referral to an Optometrist interested in visual development and functional visual problems is indicated. Initial examinations are often available via the NHS (a listing of Optometrists who have undertaken additional training in this area is available from The Secretary of The British Association of Behavioural Optometrists).

A great deal of information on visual training activities that can be used in the classroom is contained in Thinking Goes to School, by Harry Wachs & Hans Furth, and a copy of this book should be required reading for any teacher working with children with motor or developmental difficulties. It is important that posture is dealt with as soon as skews are noted, to ensure that children are writing in the most efficient mechanical positions possible. Sloping desks have been advocated by many for writing, the research on this dating as far back as 1958, yet it is rare to see this in the modern day classroom, even though the effect on visual stress levels can be significant. Appropriate pencil grip and the use of grippers have been widely discussed in this journal and should be introduced at an early stage. Good lighting giving minimal glare and adequate levels of light are also important. It is interesting that minimal lighting levels for the workplace are a statutory requirement in offices, yet schools are exempt from such restrictions.

Given the currently accepted figures that approximately thirty percent of children suffer from functional visual difficulties that are likely to affect reading, writing and classroom performance, the identification and treatment of these problems assumes major significance, and the classroom teacher is ideally placed to start the ball rolling in spotting potential problems and referring for investigation. Let us not leave this to chance.

References.

Furth, H. G. and Wachs, H. (1975) *Thinking Goes to School* New York: Oxford University Press

Harmon, D. B. (1951) *The co-ordinated Classroom.* Grand Rapids, Michigan. (This research monograph is available from The Optometric Extension Programme, 2912 S.Daimler St, Santa Anna, CA)

Optometric Extension Programme Foundation. (1980) *A Bibliography of Stress-Relieving Lens and Vision Training Research* Santa Anna California

The 1986/7 Future of Vision Development Task Force (1988) The Efficacy of Optometric Vision Therapy. *Journal of the American Optometry Association.* **59 (2),** 95-105

Walters J (1984) Portsea modified clinical technique: Results from an expanded optometric screening protocol for children. *Australian Journal of Optometry* 87-178

Ten Reference Points for Good Handwriting

Pru Wallis Myers
Handwriting Consultant

1. Handwriting, as a pattern of movement, is based on parallel down-strokes, parallel balancing up-strokes, anti-clockwise and clockwise curves that produce oval proportioned letters.

2. All lower case letters start at their top, except for 'd' and 'e'. They are all made without lifting the pen, except for 'f', 'i', 'j' and 't'.

3. The bodies of all lower case letters are the same height. Ascenders are twice as tall and descenders have 'tails' below the base line.

4. Capital letters are no taller than ascenders and need not be quite as tall.

5. Letters are evenly spaced in a joined hand through the diagonal or horizontal join line.

6. The space of an 'o' divides one word from another

7. Lines of writing are separated by at least the width of the descender space from one line together with the ascender space of the next line, given two 'body height' spaces.

8. Letters finishing on the base line join diagonally: e.g. 'e' or 'n'. Those which finish on the 'body height line' join from here: e.g. 'o' or 'w'. Descenders, such as g' can be terminal letters or they can join diagonally through a loop.

9. Any letter will join any other letter with all direction pens, but those letters ending on their lift: e.g. 'b', 'g', 'p', 's' and 'y' naturally need a pen lift or pause.

10. The pen has to be lifted after joining a few letters, to move along with the hand, as at the end of a word. The pen, hand and arm should remain in line with each other as they move along rhythmically from left to right making a pattern of movement which becomes handwriting.

When Should We Introduce Children to Joined Handwriting?

Anita Warwick
Deputy-headteacher Whitchurch First School, Harrow

"It is our policy that joined handwriting be introduced as a means of written communication on school entry. From this children are encouraged to develop a legible, free flowing script (handwriting style) of which they are suitably proud"

(From Whitchurch First School Handwriting Policy document - October 1993)

The revised National Curriculum (post Dearing) which becomes statutory in September 1995 states that:-

"At key stage 1, in handwriting pupils should be taught to hold a pencil comfortably in order to develop a legible style that follows the conventions of written English, including:-

- *writing from left to right and from top to bottom of the page;*

- *starting and finishing letters correctly;*

- *regularity of size and shape of letters;*

- *regularity of spacing of letters and words.*

*They should be taught the conventional ways of forming letters, both lower case and capitals. They should build on their knowledge of letter formation to **join letters in words**. They should develop an awareness of the importance of clear and neat presentation, in order to communicate their meaning effectively."*

It is still expected therefore that some children are capable of achieving level 3, in handwriting, at the end of key stage one. If this is the case, when should joined handwriting be introduced? Moreover, we must not lose sight of the fact that there is a considerable amount of growing evidence which clearly supports the early introduction of joined writing. During some inset sessions I have led, teachers have shared their concerns regarding the introduction of joined handwriting to 5 and 6 year olds. Is it too soon? What about letter formation? Surely it will harm their ability to read? Will they be able to both write and read joined writing? Isn't printing easier? We've always printed so why change? What about parent's reactions?

When the National Curriculum was first introduced many felt we were doing some of our children a disservice if we were not introducing them to joined writing until they reached primary school, or year 3. At this time we decided, at the school I was teaching at in Ealing, to change our handwriting policy and introduce children to joined handwriting when they first entered school. This change of policy was partly influenced by the requirements of the National Curriculum but more so by the observations that were being made in schools where joined handwriting was being introduced in the reception classes. Many were attributing an increase in creative writing, positive self esteem, the ability to write quickly and spell correctly to a joined handwriting policy on school entry.

What I would like to share with you are some of the things we have learnt; our own 6 stages of joining and the range and type of activities the children are engaged in when they first come to school.

For many years print script has been accepted as the 'natural' way to introduce children to writing. However, since the beginning of this century many have put forward quite a different argument. Now, following Dearing's proposals and the new statutory orders, many are feeling the need to review their handwriting policies and guidelines. Furthermore, it appears to make increasing sense to introduce joined writing, to children, on school entry.

From what I have seen of children's writing in the last 6 years I would find it extremely hard to revert back to a policy of printing until children reach the age of 7 or 8. It is clear for example, that joined writing follows on from the natural free writing scribbles that children make when they first come to school. It means too that there is continuity and progression throughout the school. Children are not hampered by the printing of each letter as they write. The teachers would be the first to admit to an increase in creative writing and a definite improvement in letter formation. There is also an improvement in the spacing both between letters and between words. Children also appear confident and proud that they are writing 'like an adult'. Writing has a high profile. Furthermore the parents are fully supportive and approve. The children, at the end of key stage one, are now developing their own style of joined writing. That period of regression, which for many used to happen when they changed from printing to joining, has either been eradicated or occurs in their first term or so at school. No longer do you hear "how do I join these letters?" or "I can't write like that?".

What we are doing, when they enter school, is introducing the children to a style of writing. We are training them in good habits from the very beginning. We are helping them to develop their motor skills by giving them regular daily exercise. Handwriting is indeed an art, and daily practice is necessary if we are to develop and perfect this art.

WHAT DO WE DO IN THE RECEPTION CLASSES?

First of all, even before a child has been accepted for a place at the school, we give parents a copy of our handwriting model and guidelines on how to help their child. If parents are informed early enough many of the bad habits some children have developed, before they enter school, can be eradicated.

We recognise that children pass through developmental stages. These are:-
- the pre-writing pattern stage;
- producing separate letters stage;
- producing letters and linking them to their growing knowledge of sounds;
- beginning to join letters in words and writing their own name;
- producing joined writing with confidence;
- developing a personalised hand;

In any one class (at Whitchurch First School), you may find children at any one of these developmental stages.

We **do** teach individual letter formation. We combine work on letter formation with sounds, handwriting practice and patterns work. When we teach letter formation it is useful to group letters together. Below is a list of suggested groupings based on similar movements:-

c ~ c o a g d q

i ~ i u l t y

r ~ r m h b p

x ~ x v w z

e f j k s

Once children have been introduced to individual letters we move on to 2 and then 3 letter words. In each of our reception and year one classrooms we introduce a new word each week in, what we hope, is a fun way! This enables children to practice the spelling and the handwriting join(s) at the same time. In this way we are able to introduce children to all the following stages of joining by the end of year 1.

HANDWRITING - OUR 'JOINING' POLICY

As I see it , there are 6 stages of joining. These are:-

Stage 1 - Baseline to top of small letter and straight down e.g. *in, an, am*
Stage 2 - Baseline to top of ascender and straight down e.g. *it, all*
Stage 3 - Baseline to top of small letter and back round e.g. *is, as, so, do*
Stage 4 - Top of small letter to top of ascender e.g. *of, hot*
Stage 5 - Horizontal joins e.g *or, on*
Stage 6 - Double letter joins e.g. *ll, ss, ff*

I introduced these 6 stages to enable us to link together both handwriting practice, practice in the different types of joins and spelling. Moreover, the words carry meaning. The teachers and children are able to put the words into context - they are not isolated letters just joined together to give children practice at a particular type of join (as is evident in some handwriting schemes).

OTHER ACTIVITIES THAT ARE TAKING PLACE IN THE RECEPTION CLASSES

- In the child's writing book - the children all '**have a go**' at writing first . The teacher will (generally no more than once a week) ask the child for his/her permission to show them how to write what they have written in a joined up style of writing. Then, the child will, depending on what stage he/she is at, either write over the top of the teacher's model or underneath. As the child progresses we will pick just a few words to practice, often choosing the ones that **are** spelt correctly.

- Look, cover, write, check is used, as a method to help a child spell frequently used words. Children do require careful supervision if they are to use this method.

- Tracing their name - but do watch carefully and help.

- Making letter shapes. Glueing pasta/string onto letter shapes/words. Writing their name in a tray filled with dry sand. Trace over sandpaper letters

- Practice forming individual letters correctly.

- Joining together letters, to make a pattern

- Tracing and drawing patterns from left to right.

- Joining together 2 letters, to make a word.

- Each classroom has a writing corner - children are able to experiment with a variety of pens and pencils. Free writing is encouraged. The children make their own books, birthday cards, lists etc

- See adults writing.

- Copying. A line from a nursery rhyme/poem.

- Using small chalkboards and chalks. Using small whiteboards and waterbased pens.

- Threading beads, sewing, art and craft activites, plasticine, model making, clay and play dough - all help to aid the development of hand control and finer motor skills.

- Following words in a book with a finger.

- Sequencing picures to tell a story.

- Word games.

- See the handwriting model around them - on coat pegs, drawer labels, wall and table displays.

- Verbalising the direction of movement when writing e.g. up, down, across, over.

- Children **are** given guidelines - at least some of the time - to help them.

A HANDWRITING MODEL

A good handwriting model is essential with clear exit strokes. Exit strokes lead the writer to the point where the next letter begins, which aids letter formation and helps develop fluency, legibility and speed. It is important that the whole school is aware of the model and the school's joining policy i.e.which letters join and which ones, if any, do not.

Consistency and continuity are important. We need to allow and encourage children to progress at their own rate and build on their developing skills. In the early stages it is, I feel, so important that we are encouraging children to join, with all the positive benefits this entails.

The model we use has been reviewed and updated 3 times in the last 3 years. I am not afraid to admit to this! All staff have been able to have an inpuit and the model has changed in the light of our experience. For example, originally our model was based on letters joining from the baseline. This however encouraged some childen into a bad habit when they wrote certain words e.g. an *a* linked to *m* to form the word *am*. Instead of going from the bottom of the **a**, up to the top of the **m** and back down, then up and over, they went from the bottom of the letter *a* then up and over. Our new policy states that most letters have clearly defined exit strokes which helps children to join from the top. This I feel has helped eradicate this early, quite visible problem.

It is important to encourage children to join together as many letters as possible. Every time they lift their pen/pencil from the paper they have to decide where to start the next letter.

SOME THINGS WE HAVE LEARNT

1. Teachers are amazingly adaptable - we have to be!

2. We all have our own personal style.

3. There is always a period of regression when there is a change from printing to cursive writing.

4. Teaching joined writing from the beginning really does aid letter formation.

5. Joined handwriting enables a natural space to occur both between letters and between words.

6. We have seen no evidence at all that joined handwriting, may in some way, hamper reading.

7. Research evidence strongly supports our handwriting policy.

8. Parents must be informed a.s.a.p.

9. Be wary of handwriting schemes - we found it more useful to build up our own resources.

10.A handwriting policy must be a whole school policy - or else it won't work! Also its unfair on the children, parents and other staff.

11.Joined writing must be written clearly.

12.Lots of individual and small group work is essential. Watch children writing and let them watch you.

13. Aids spelling - linking handwriting practice to spelling (grouping words in families) really helps.

14. A sloping surface does help - especially those children with poor motor skills. (Stick together and cover 2, now obsolete, N.C. folders!).

15. Children will join letters together when they are ready - and not (as was often the case in the past), when we think they are ready.

16. Daily practice pays off! Even if it's just 10 minutes - writing their own name etc.

17. A joined handwriting policy, on school entry, aids progression. It is no longer necessary to change from printing to joining. We are building on the pre-writing/scribble patterns children first make when they come to school.

18. There is an increased awareness of the structure of words - children seem more able to see words as a whole.

19. It is important for the child to see both the moving and the static model.

20. Children appear to exhibit both an increase in confidence and competency throughout the school.

21. There is an increase in positive self-esteeem (amongst *all* the children). They feel they are doing adult writing.

22. There is a built in progression which is aided by our joining policy and our 6 stages of joining guidelines.

23. Inform supply teachers - give them a copy of the handwriting model.

24. Stories seem longer. Creative writing has improved.

25. Speed and fluency have improved. Joined writing helps children write as quickly as they want to.

26. We have eliminated the problem of changing from print script to joining in Year 3, and all the associated problems this entailed.

27. All staff <u>now</u> share the same opinion - we would not want to return to a policy of printing!

Finally, I do not see myself as any kind of an expert on writing. All I hope to be able to do is to share my own experience, and that of other teachers. My aim is to help others as they undertake, or consider undertaking a review of their handwriting policies and guidelines in their school.

References

Cripps, C. and Cox, R. (1989) *Joining the ABC*. Wisbech: LDA

Jarman, C. (1991) *The development of handwriting skills.* Hemel Hempstead: Simon and Schuster

Sassoon, R. (1990) *Handwriting: a New Perspective*. Cheltenham: Stanley Thornes

Sassoon, R. (1990) *Handwriting: the Way to teach it*. Cheltenham: Stanley Thornes

Handwriting Hints: Advice from an Uncoordinated Writer of Italic

Kate Gladstone
New York

This is intended as a follow-up to Miss Hastings' excellent articles in the *Handwriting Review 1993* which drew my attention because her difficulties and life-story are startlingly similar to my own. So much so that I will not try anyone's patience with recounting them just now. I thought that she, and perhaps others with difficulties like hers, might like to hear from someone across the Atlantic. Someone who, as it happens, handled the handwriting (but not other) difficulties and malco-ordinations by careful study and use of Italic handwriting. Italic may be old to you, but it is scarcely heard of here; I came upon it only by the merest chance.

Before I go into the question of style at all, I'd like to corroborate and add to Miss Hastings' remarks upon handwriting in general.

POSTURE AND COMFORT

She rightly considers these essential. I have found that one way of helping to assure them is to use, on one's chair, the sort of pillow that can often be bought from makers of products to avoid or remedy back pain. The best kind of pillow is the kind that is designed to be quite firm, and to be a couple of inches higher in the back than in the front. In fact, it looks a lot like a sloping board, only softer, smaller and not hollow. This automatically puts the spine in a correct and comfortable position. Such commercially available pillows often have washable covers and (more importantly) ties to attach them to the back of the chair. Lacking a commercially made pillow, one can always make one or have one made.

An equal or greater posture help is, as many of us will know from recent *Handwriting Review* articles, a sloping board. These need not be expensive; I have seen excellent 'home-made' ones, including one that was a simple sheet of hard plastic, bent to provide an angle.

Failing such a board - or if, as with many of us, your desk is cluttered with papers or you somehow always end up writing away from it - you may consider acquiring what is known as a 'lap desk'. These are often obtainable in large stationers' and also sometimes (less pretty but no less costly) from suppliers of products for disabled persons, or again, they can be made at home; all a lap desk is, is a wide, thick pillow with a biggish board mounted on it.

Or again, when without either a lap desk or a sloping desk top, why not just rest your notebook against the edge of a conventional table or desk.

Also, I have found that pressing <u>firmly</u> on the writing paper with the <u>non-writing</u> hand helps posture and also relieves tension and excessive pressure in the writing hand.

PENS

I would agree with what Ms Hastings recommends; i.e. broad barrels and long, easily visible nibs, as well as with two of her specific brand name recommendations: Fisher Space Pen and Sheaffer No-Nonsense.

I'd like, though, to add the following: For a ball-point or roller ball pen, the broader the point the better. Most ball points and roller balls, though, are unfortunately made only in Extra-Fine, Fine and/or Medium sizes; even the medium is a shade too small to control easily. It somehow does not grip the paper as well as something broader. Happily though, both the Fisher Space Pen ball point refill and the Parker Jotter ball pen refill are also made in Broad size. These almost always have to be ordered directly from the firm because they are far less in demand. Stationers seldom carry them and mostly are unaware of their existence. As to Roller-balls, a good broad point exists in the Pentel Rolling Writer. (The Rolling Writer, though is what they call for some reason 'disposable' - meaning that one has to dispose of it (not refill it) at the end of it's useful life. Also, the plastic barrel, though ideal in terms of grip, has to some eyes a gimcrackish or juvenile look and is a little too lightweight for everyone's hand). Fibre tip or plastic based markers are good too, when the situation permits, as are disposable, technical pens, which have permanent, non-smudging ink (do such pens exist in the UK?) - the broader pointed the better. (I prefer an 0.07mm tip - the same as I like in mechanical pencils).

Ordinary fat pointed writing tools (e.g. broad fountain pens) are very good, but I find that using a thick-and-thin pen or marker (such as are sold for calligraphy or italic handwriting) is even better, if its of good quality and not too narrow or sharp. The extra control it lends the hand lasts, in my experience, even into subsequent use of an ordinary pen; for instance, when I have to put down my favourite fountain pen to make out a multi-part copy form with a ball point.

The Sheaffer No-Nonsense pen range does include a 'Sheaffer Calligraphy Set' which contains three italic nibs that work well for me (the Fine one, which I like best, is about like a Broad from most other italic pen makers). But this pen tends to leak a bit when carried about in a handbag; so probably more practical are the Pentel 'Italic Fountain Markers' and, for fountain-pen writers, the Parker Calligraphy Pens which are leakproof in my experience and also superbly smooth writers.

I have tried a variety of gripping-aids. One of the best is a simple soft-plastic sleeve to slide over the pencil, like a hollow cylindrical cushion. Moulded ones such as the 'Stetro' or the three sided wedge work just as well, but tend to constrain the hand, so that after writing it is difficult initially (for me at least) to unlock my hand and fingers for non-writing activities. My hand, though not cramped or otherwise painful, seems reluctant to change the position it has been kept in. However, these more constraining aids (especially the Stetro) do make it easier to handwrite at length than a sleeve-like (or no) aid does. One problem; I have not yet found a small pen-gripping aid which can conveniently be used with a pen that has a cap. This means that gripping-aids cannot be used with fountain pens and many ball points and roller-balls; a loss.

I find that my handwriting often improves with various specially made pencils or pens, the kinds that are sold through medical catalogues to people with hand injuries and the like, but I'll not discuss them here as I do not know how easily they are available to all *Handwriting Reveiw* readers. Also, the great variety of such devices merits for them a complete article devoted entirely to that subject.

PRACTICE RECOMMENDATIONS:

I wholly endorse Miss Hastings' remarks. However, I would like to add the following:

The 15 minutes a day can with advantage be extended to 20, **if** the period is broken up into multiple daily sessions of five to ten minutes, no longer. One may wish to set a times, or arrange for another person to call you when time is up. Then one does not have to think 'how much longer?'

In my opinion, something that Miss Hastings does not mention, which is quite helpful, is that one ought to have a model to work from. In fact it is often helpful to buy two of whatever model, copybook etc. one is using; one to look at, one to write in. This leaves the letter models intact in one book while permitting you to trace and copy the models in the other book. The books are both opened to the page being worked on and stacked one within the other.

The book to be written in ('writing' book) is within the other ('model') book; as writing progresses from line to line, successive lines of the 'model' book should be exposed to view by holding the 'writing' book down and sliding the 'model' book up a bit.

If the books are at all bulky it is of course better to have xeroxes of the required pages serve in the stead of the 'writing' book; these also serve as a convenient bookmark, so that you do not have to turn pages at the start of each practice session to find where you left off last time.

Tracing is at least as important as copying. I would recommend tracing a letter or word correctly in the 'writing' book at least five times before copying it from the model book. Trace a letter or, later on, a word, at least this often, then copy it, then look at what you did; then go and trace the next letter or word. Don't, just at first, trace a whole sentence through before you copy it; the motor image of the writing won't be distinct by the time you go back and copy what you traced. By 'look at what you did' I mean: Look at your writing to see all the ways in which the letter shapes do not resemble the model. Then, perhaps on a separate piece of paper (another advantage of copying the copybook) write the letter or worked so that it looks much more like the model - repeat until you think it is visibly much better.

Many of us with handwriting problems do not naturally practice effectively - either we do not see any difference between the model and our attempts: knowing that ours is wrong or unacceptably different only because others tell us so, or (though we see the difference between our attempts and the model), we simply do not see in what these differences consist, or see how to make our writing closer to the model.

When this happens, I have found that (for whatever reason) it is very helpful not to think of the letter itself, but of the blank spaces within and between the letters; to think of making thesem not the letters themselves, come out as they did in the model. For instance, you wouldn't think 'I've got to make the 'a' look like whats in the book'; you'd think 'how does this **space** right **here** look? And what will make it come out the same in my writing'? I don't know why this should work better, but it often does.

Not only is it very helpful (I would even say needful) to select a specific model of writing (as opposed to 'I've got to do better; my n's look too much like u's or some such) it's also a very good idea to select a model which you consider will pose you the last possible difficulties.

For instance, I selected italic as a model, rather that just working to perfect one of the styles I'd been taught at school, because I had all of my life had difficulty specifically with features of the school styles that do not exist in the italic style.

If you do not have very clear ideas of what is easy or difficult for you as a writer, you can find out and select a style to suit by taking a pencil or dry pen and repeatedly tracing over models of different styles of handwriting - not only alphabet exemplars, but worked and sentences, e.g from a copybook. Start slowly and then go faster and faster. The higher a speed you can reach (without departing form the model) and the fewer difficult motions or trouble spots you run into, the more likely that the model you are test driving is one you will find pleasant and possible for you.

About italic and its close kin (Gourdie's Simple Modern Hand, Jarman's Basic Modern Hand, etc) I do think that this is a very good option for uncoordinated people, both young and old.

I am not insisting on a fussy italic, or even on an edged pen, unless the edged pen helps you write (as it does me) and the results are more pleasant and clearer to others and to yourself.

The aim, I think, especially for the uncoordinated writer, should not be for ordinary handwriting to appear 'fancy' or 'calligraphic' or 'historic' - it should be to write a clear, practical hand which just happens to avoid shapes and motions which are 'trouble spots' (i.e. particular complex sequences of motions which are specially difficult for the uncoordinated writer, even after much practice to make them habitual and to reproduce them (especially at speed) as neatly and distinguishably as they need to be) and to favour shapes that make it possible to retain legibility at high speeds, rather that other shapes (as easy, or possibly easier to learn initially) that decay at high speeds.

Enough has been written about italic that I need not go over all that is found in its favour. However, I think the unco-ordinated writer who selects italic as a model should stay away (just at first) from Fairbank's *Handwriting Manual*. This will be very useful to him/her later - when s/he has acquired some scribal skill - but Fairbank assumes that the reader is normal in manual dexterity, co-ordination, and the ability to teach his/her nerves and muscles new tricks. Similarly, the little leaflets that come with most italic pen sets are not much help. Because of their brevity they do not provide much practice material or guidance, and they tend to be more calligraphically oriented than is appropriate for a beginner, especially one with handwriting problems.

How would you select a good italic book if you were an uncoordinated person who had chosen italic as his/her model? I would look for one which started off with writing patterns resembling scribble and establish these firmly before going on to evolve them into letters. The book should also handle writing with joins, and the development of speed in writing, well before introducing the edged pen.

Also, the book should not imply that you must want (and be able) to do edged-pen writing in order to do 'real' italic. The examples of italic handwriting that it gives (and the more, by different writers, the better) should show italic done well with different sorts of writing instruments. It should also go into details in teaching how to use an edged pen; many authors seem to assume that you can just pick it up and it will write for you.

This is not true for us uncoordinated people. Even where the pen hold looks right something about it will usually be 'off' - if only to a degree that is imperceptible (and possibly immaterial) when one is writing with an ordinary pen, but will prevent the pen from writing if it is edged. It can take weeks (or months) for a grossly uncoordinated person to conquer this, and not every one will want to bother.

A final note about children. Miss Hastings does not give any special advice to children or their parents, although she does note that her handwriting difficulties existed while she was a child, and does recommend that children should be taught to write well in early life.

There is now no dearth of advice (some good, some less so) on handwriting for children with difficulties, though I have not seen any handwriting models described as being designed specially for the uncoordinated child or adult. Advice on dysgraphia, and dyspraxia in general, is easy to get in the UK, judging from the *Handwriting Review*, but in the USA, though the problems are recognised to some degree, such advice hardly any resources exist. Such things are needed though, as anyone who has an unusually poor handwriter in school can tell you.

The less normally coordinated a child or adult is, the less likely it is that the materials, practice time etc. designed for (and sufficient to) the normally coordinated person will be enough for this 'odd (wo)man out'. And it is as well to note (in designing handwriting methods for the un co-ordinated) that there will be a difference between adults and children using a given method.

An adult has freedom to select his/her own handwriting style according to what s/he needs and likes. For instance, if s/he dislikes added loops or total joining up, no one will make him/her use them. But a child is likely to be subjected to school demands to write in the style the school approves, whether or not s/he can adapt to it.

I know only one case in which a child (normally coordinated, I think) successfully resisted the style the school demanded and was allowed to be exempt from there on; and that child had powerful support - he's the grandson of Tom Gourdie!

In the USA at least, many teachers value student's attempts, however unsuccessful, to conform with the desired style much more than they do the actual success of writing.

Students coming to the USA from other countries using different styles (or even children who had been taught a differing style at home or, sometimes quite successfully, copied some italic or other 'unacceptable' style they'd seen) have been told that, yes, their handwriting in the 'wrong' style was admittedly far faster, clearer and more attractive than anything they (or most of their classmates or teachers) could produce in the 'right' style but still, even though it was better, they'd have to give it up. No one (except the children involved) seemed to think that this was peculiar or ill-considered.

This is hard enough on ordinary children, but it is much, much harder on the uncoordinated. We have great difficulty forming, then acting on, the mental images of movements, and the images do not become habit, then 'second nature' as seems to happen with other people (or at least this does not happen nearly as quickly or reliably). So the difficulties of an enforced change in style of any sort are immense for us; the more different the required model is from what was taught before (or from what can help the writer), the more the muscular images become confused and confusing.

Reader, if you happen to be an uncoordinated child (or his/her Mum or Dad) and specific features of the school method are causing trouble, you may have to suffer a less than ideal method or go as far as to change schools for this reason. Fighting a school on this can be very difficult; often the teachers who claim most loudly 'we don't care how students write, just so its legible' are the very ones to say, when confronted with excellent but different writing, 'That's is not how to write!'

Children with such little freedom in the choice of a handwriting style may just have to practice an unsuitable (at least for them) method as well as they can (hoping it will be taught well, with attention to those essentials of good writing that are common to all styles and need to be attended to be all writers, well or ill co-ordinated), and be helped (perhaps by out of school tutors or other specialists) to select and practice something more suitable later on, at whatever stage their school ceases to teach or demand a particular kind of writing.

Book Reviews

The early 1990s saw a plethora of new publications related to handwriting and handwriting schemes. Many of these were described in the 1993 edition of Handwriting Review. This year, as readers will see, far fewer publications relating solely to handwriting have emerged, and many of the new publications instead concentrate on specific learning difficulties and reading.

As always, I would be delighted to hear of any new publications which readers wish us to review or indeed of anyone who would like to write reviews for this section.

Naomi Hartnell
Reviews Editor.

Wallis Myers, P. (1994) *Movement into Writing.* Available from: P. Wallis Myers, 2 Richmond Court, Richmond Road. Bowdon, Altrincham. WA14 2TZ

Many handwriting schemes have been published since 1989, or so, in response to National Curriculum requirements for the teaching and assessment of handwriting in schools. In many respects, this publication is rather late in the publication sequence, as many schools have policies on the teaching of handwriting already established. This is unfortunate, as the Wallis Myers publications are the result of years of personal research and practice on the part of the author. Prue was in turn an art teacher, an HMI for art and primary education, and always a voluntary worker in schools, which she continued until the time of publication. She is well versed in the history of handwriting, and knew personally the early authorities and writers on the subject. The scheme has been well tried with pupils in the 4 to 11 year age range.

The major element of the scheme is a 200 page handbook, 'Movement into Writing'. The aim is to establish cursive letters which will form the foundation for a running hand when the pupil reaches secondary school. Print script is avoided, so that the return to print script, which many secondary pupils experience, can be avoided. Letter joins and lower loops are encouraged, when letter formation has become well established. The author deals with all general questions the teacher is likely to ask. For example, there are sections on posture, letter patterns and movements, and extensive discussion about the hand and its role in the management of modern pens. Teachers will welcome the photocopiable pupil worksheets which number 100, or more, and range from letter pattern practice, to consonant blends, and to letter strings such as 'ill', 'all, and 'ing'.

Figure 1. P. Wallis Myers 'Movement into Writing model

Nursery child's flow line

There are three supplementary elements to the scheme, which consist of:

The *Animal Alphabet Story Book*, suitable for pre-school and Reception class children. This attractive book has 56 pages, with facing pages consisting of animal illustrated letter, which the child can trace over, colour in, and learn, and a story to interest and encourage memorising the letter and its movement.

The set of 100 large, moveable letters can be used to develop correct letter formation, alphabet skills, and word building. The letters are each approximately 10 inches tall, and of varying width, according to the letter. They are attractive white on royal blue, and suitably laminated for hardwear in the home, nursery, or classroom.

The sloping board is simply made, stackable, and covered in a durable material, which is pleasant to handle and to write upon.

I recommend all elements of this comprehensive and well thought out scheme. However, there will be readers who have a use for individual items, each of which can be purchased separately.

The Handwriting Manual, £15.00 + p+p; *The animal Alphabet Story Book*, £5.00 + p+p; Large Moveable Letters, £10.00 + p+p; The Sloping Board £8.00 + p+p

Jean Alston
Author and Consulting Psychologist

Fidge,L.(1993) *Handwriting in Context*. Folens Publishers Ltd. 4 Resource Books. ISBN 1 8527 3922/3930/3949/3957. Pbk. £17.95 each book.

Handwriting in Context is a photocopiable resource in four books, spanning four stages of learning to write. Each book has the same very important four page introduction of rationale and teaching points, thereby enabling teachers to buy only the book or books they want without missing significant general information and instructions on the teaching of handwriting.

Then follow two pages of notes about the material in the particular book and then over fifty pages of photocopiable material. I liked the attractive presentation, format and the gradations in the teaching steps very much indeed, and was particularly impressed with the pre-writing material in Book 1. The recommended starting age of 5 years however could, I feel be lowered to 3 since many children are being taught to write letters before they are 5 without the benefits of the excellent pre-writing exercises in Book 1.

The material in all the books is very user friendly and I feel sure that most children, if guided sympathetically [and individually, as far as is possible] through this material, will learn to write easily, competently and enthusiastically. The assessment pages are particularly useful and it is to be hoped that the teacher will be knowledgeable enough to pick out children having difficulty and provide extra and suitable practice for them. I would have liked a little more help to have been given with handwriting problems since self-assessment, although a very valuable aid to improvement, cannot replace a teacher's expert knowledge.

I liked the variety of exercises in each book, and especially the concept of filling in letters, enabling whole pages of 'writing' to be produced, which look attractive but have not put undue strain on a beginning writer. I also liked the comparison of handwriting styles in Book 4, encouraging pupils to become aware of their own style of writing. Encouragement of awareness of presentation is very welcome but rightly reserved for book 4 when pupils have become confident and fast writers.

There are so many excellent aspects of this material that I was disappointed to find that the author had described only one style of cursive writing, namely semi-joined and with most letters starting at the top with exit strokes only. It is not until Book 4 that he introduces alternative ways of forming joined letters, and asks pupils to choose which they prefer. This is too late, since by Book 4 most pupils will have formed the habit of writing as they were first taught.

I do not wish to enter into the fully-joined-cursive-with-loops versus the semi-joined controversy, but it would have been so useful for teachers who want to teach the former to have had the benefits of this excellent manual at their disposal. As a teacher with some experience of teaching children with handwriting and reading problems I know the benefits that entry strokes and loops can give to children who have difficulty in remembering how to form letters from left to right and then to progress from left to right across the page. It would be extremely helpful if another four books could be brought out with exercises designed for this style. I am quite sure that they would be greatly welcomed, not only by bodies like the Dyslexia Association but also by teachers of children with lesser but still significant problems. I would greatly look forward

Pat Moseley
Special Needs Support Teacher, Mid Glamorgan

Jarman, C. (1993) *Handwriting Skills. Photocopy Masters Books 1, 2 and 3. A4.* Cheltenham: Stanley Thornes. Book 1. 32 pp £12.99; Book 2. 48 pp. £15.00; Book 3. 48 pp. £15.00.

Although many materials to assist the teaching of handwriting have been published in recent years, there are few that one would unreservedly recommend. This hesitation occurs because the style they adopt is unlikely to establish for pupils a functional cursive style that will carry them through to secondary education. However, I have few reservations about Christopher Jarman's Handwriting Skills Copybook Masters, which have many attributes which members of the handwriting world would expect to find in a well thought out scheme. Movement is built into the model from the beginning, and the static movements encouraged through teaching upright print script, do not occur in this programme. The forward sloping line, and the anticlockwise oval movement are intrinsic to every exercise.

The programme begins with large maze patterns in which line drawing and anticlockwise oval movements are frequent. The cursive (joined) and other handwriting simulation patterns follow in Book 1. Progress to good letter forms, short words, numerals and capital letters occur in Book 2. Most letters have no exit strokes at the beginning of *Book 2* just 'l' and 't', but letter joins are encouraged in short word copying. By the end of the book, exit strokes appear on letters such as 'd', 'l', 'm' and 'n'. Book 3 has a fully cursive, slightly sloping script that should take pupils on to develop relatively fluent handwriting.

Christopher Jarman has been asked on several occasions why he does not introduce exit strokes to the first letters that children learn. His intention is to establish reliable letter forms before extensive writing demands are made on young writers. However, on page 41 of Book 2, letters such as 'n' and 'm' have no exit strokes for joining, whereas on page 43 the exit strokes are introduced without explanation or preparation. Long, across the page, letter patterns are given in Book 1, and full line length patterns are presented in Book 3. Many believe that to copy long patterns, without pause, serves no useful purpose. And why, one might ask, are pupils required to copy long sentences in Latin, French, German and Spanish in Book 3? However, I am sure that Jarman has his reasons for this exercise. Perhaps the young writer is required to concentrate on letter joins, rather than meaning, at this stage.

Figure 1 . Exercise from Page 41, Book 2

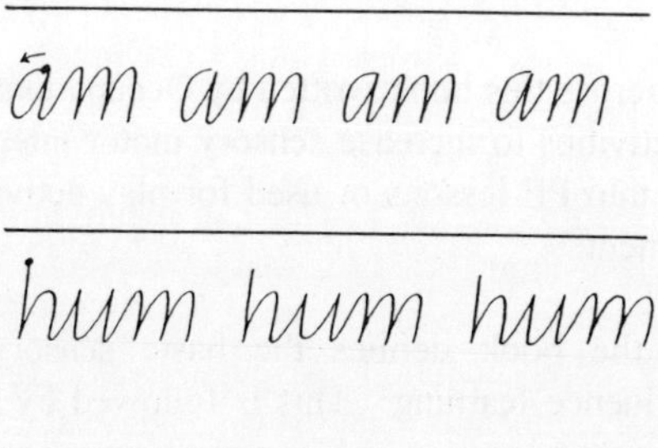

Figure 2 . Exercise from Page 43, Book 2

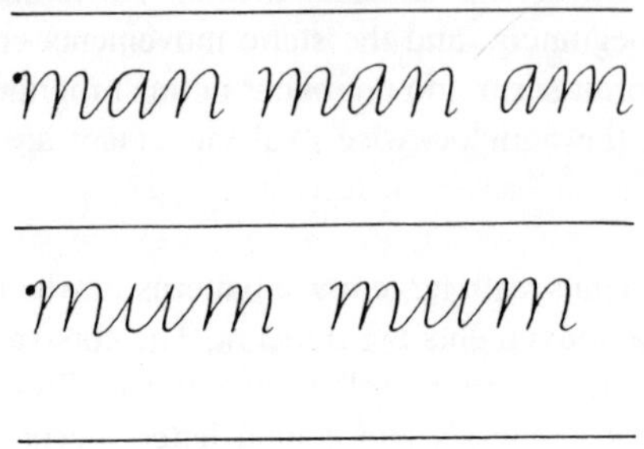

man man am

mum mum

Readers should note that Jarman does not advocate joins from certain letters to those which follow. Letters which do not join are 'b', 'p', 'g', 'j', 'y' and 's', because in these letters the final stroke is leftwards. These Photocopy Masters and Jarman's Handwriting Copybooks 1-6, are intended to be used in conjunction with *The Development of Handwriting Skills: A resource Book for Teachers*, also available from Stanley Thornes.

Jarman, C. *The Development of Handwriting Skills: A resource book for teachers*. £16.00
Jarman, C. *Handwriting Skills Copybooks, 1-6*. £2.50 each paperback

Jean Alston
Author andConsulting Psychologist

Bissell, J., Fisher, J., Owens, G. and Polcyn, P. (1988) *Sensory Motor Handbook - A Guide For Implementing and Modifying Activities in the Classroom.* Sensory Motor International Publishers, 1402 Cravens Avenue, Torrance, California 90501. $29.00 + $2.90 Postage. Payment must be in dollars.

I have only just come across this book written by Occupational Therapists. It is full of ideas of activities to increase sensory motor integration which could be incorporated into PE lessons or used for play activities all using the minimum of equipment.

The first section of the book defines the basic sensory and motor components which influence learning. This is followed by strategies for modifying activities and then looking at the problems in each sensory~motor area and giving 'have your tried' ideas. Over a hundred activities are then described, with details of the equipment needed, a description of the game or activity, what the teacher should notice about the child's performance and a simple picture of the stick children performing the game which livens up the text. The games are divided up into several sections e.g. Ball and Balloon games, Skipping Rope games. At the beginning of each section a chart indicates the primary sensory and motor component to be found in each activity. In the appendix details on making the equipment is given and music for the tunes suggested is provided.

This book would be an extremely useful resource for anyone working with children with development coordination disorder.

Jane Taylor
Handwriting Therapis/ Consultant

Wolfe, R.(1987) *Learn to Cut - A structured programme of cutting task with reproducible patterns*. Communication Skill Builders Inc, 3830 E.Bellevue/PO Box 42050, Tuscon, Arizona 85733. $29.00.

Learn to Cut is a series of photocopiable sheets to assist the teaching of the skill of cutting. The programme is devided into two sections.

In Part 1 programme, the task is broken down into eight Skill Steps. Each Step commences with a pre-test, which later can be used as a post-test), to ascertain the appropriate starting level. The first Step is to cut a line $1/4$"wide, 1" long, stopping at the designated length, with 80° accuracy. The line is black so it is easy for the child to observe whether s/he is cutting accurately. The next step is to cut out a shape which is stuck on to a fun, simple, clearly outlined in bold print picture. For example, a cut out square forms the box for Jack in the Box, part of a book cover which a girl is reading or a clown's top hat. An additional activity would be to colour the completed picture. Squares, rectangles, triangles and diamonds shapes follow with the line width reduced to $1/8$". The Steps progress to circles, ovals, crescents, hearts, and stars. A record sheet is provided.

The second section consists of 61 cutting activities with a variety of pictures to construct using the cut out shapes.

This would be a very useful resource for a busy classroom teacher as it provides a structured frame work of activities for a child with poor scissors skills. It is an activity which could be done at home with the parents supervising.

Jane Taylor
Handwriting Therapist/Consutant

Bell, Christopher (1993) *Helping young children to become writers*. Crediton, Devon: Southgate. 63pp, £7.95

This book is one of the most recent to be written by a member of the 'emergent writing' educational camp. It is well written, with the message succinctly stated by Christopher Bell, its enthusiastic author. Bell's major message is that authorship should be encouraged in all children. Everything they draw or write is of value and shows the teacher what the child knows; a view with which none of us should disagree. With encouragement, young writers' progress through the stages that Bell has discerned, similar to the way in which they develop inventive spelling, for which Gentry has become so well known. They are:

STAGE 1: Invention, randomness and imitation
STAGE 2: From randomness to the beginning of order and phonic
        awareness
STAGE 3: Progress towards conventional writing

The author presents lists of features to be found in each stage of writing development. For example, at Stage 1, there will be little differentiation between pictures and writing, but there may be early use of left to right, top to bottom and other basic conventions. The teacher's role is not to offer the correct transposition or to model, but to encourage pupils to participate in interactive class writing, even if they have few skills with which to do so. Each contribution is accepted and left for all pupils to see and to read back. Children are also taught to work in pairs, reading their own writing to each other, and asking partners for help whenever they need it. The teacher is left to deal with other thins, or to work with other groups, and the queue at the teacher's desk is avoided. It needs courage to adopt this policy, and Bell has obviously needed to risk criticism from parents and grandparents. However, he justifies all he writes, and presents examples of individual pupils' writing over a period, to prove his point.

Although much of this text is about encouraging letter sounds, rather than their movements, and Bell makes those sounds inappropriately, allowing an unnecessary 'schwa' to sound with virtually every letter, he does make some concessions to handwriting. Each child has an alphabet strip, which is made by the child and renewed at the beginning of each new topic. However, letter starting points are not presented on these letters. There is a chart, on which each letter does show its starting point, to show how letters fall into groups with regard to movement, but it is not clear how each child is made aware of the importance of these conventions. The writing of the children he uses to illustrate Stage 3 development are still showing signs of inaccurate letter formation and weak concepts of relative letter size. One would need to examine writing of the same pupils at top primary and lower secondary school levels, and across the ability range, to be fully convinced about this approach to writing development.

Two aspects of this policy concern me. None of the pupils is introduced to lined paper and one wonders how they learn about alignment and relative letter and letter part size, in consequence. One also wonders whether the movement principle, 'practice makes permanent (rather than perfect)' operates for these pupils. If it does, they will have great difficulty in relinquishing the incorrect movements that they have inevitably practised in the early stages of their writing. Bell suggests that writing is developmental, as are speaking and walking, which is clearly not the case. Less able pupils, in particular, will need much more instructive intervention than the author suggests.

This book is worthy of attention. It is an attractively presented book, easy to digest, and all readers will gain some information from its pages. Those who believe themselves convinced that the more traditional approaches to teaching handwriting offer greater benefit to pupils, should nevertheless know what their critics advocate. We can only gain through greater awareness and dialogue. This book provides an easy and interesting contribution to the debate. Many aspects of Christopher Bell's philosophy are well justified and cannot easily be dismissed.

Reference

Gentry, J. R. (1981) Learning to Spell Developmentally. *Reading Teacher*, **34**, 378-81. (182)

Jean Alston
Author andConsulting Psychologist

Walton, J. (1994) *Golden Key Spelling Rules*! 146pp. ISBN 1 874757 09 7- Teacher's Book £16.50.
Walton, J. (1992*) The Golden Key: Spelling by Singing Volumes 1 and 2* + tape £5.99 each.
Children's Work Book - The Golden Key Spelling by Singing Volume 1 and 2 + tape £5.99 each.
All published by H. A. Walton, 28, Mandeville Road, Hertford, SG13 8J

The Golden Key spelling activities include a set of books with difficult spellings set to music, accompanied by tapes. The other resources cover spelling rules and include work books and a photocopiable resource book. The idea being to offer a multisensory approach to learning spellings, especially the high frequency key words. The emphasis is on ensuring automatic memory by tracing over words to be learnt and following this activity with exercises. The tracing could also be combined with handwriting practice. The work books are clear and helpful with many fun activities. They are suitable for fairly able five to nine year olds experiencing difficulties. The Spelling Rules are aimed at KS2 pupils. There seemed to be rather too much information on a page for pupils who are experiencing difficulties with literacy acquisition, but could be a useful tool for teaching rules to pupils experiencing less severe difficulties. The second section had some good ideas for activities and teaching through mnemonics. This is not a complete spelling scheme, but will aid pupils who are experiencing difficulties to learn in an interesting way.

Brenda Manning
Base Leader Base for Specific Learning Difficulties Watford, Herts.

Cort, C. (1994) *The Reading Activities Resource Bank*. Blueprints Series. Cheltenham: Stanley Thornes. ISBN 0-7487 1730 7
Hadley, H.(1994) *The Phonics Book*. Blueprints Series. Cheltenham: Stanley Thornes. ISBN 0-7487 1729 3. £10.99.

The Reading Activities Resource Bank will be a welcome addition to the photocopiable resources of any infant school. The vocabulary is compatible with a number of popular reading schemes and covers the common sight vocabulary. The games are fun and the illustrations bright and appealing. It allows the classroom teacher to have relevant, carefully graded activities at a fraction of the cost of commercially produced materials.

The Phonics Book is also a photocopiable resource. It has an excellent introduction covering phonic theory and each section has a clear explanation as to its application. Each single sound has a section showing the distinct direction for letter formation and a practice section. This ensures that sound/symbol awareness is raised, together with good inbuilt handwriting practice and reinforcement.

Brenda Manning
Base Leader Base for Specific Learning Difficulties Watford, Herts.

Lloyd S and Wernham S. (1993) *Finger Phonics. Books 1-7*. Jolly Learning Ltd., Clare Hall, Chapel Lane, Chigwell, Essex. £19.50 for set of 7 books.

These books, published a year ago by Jolly Learning, are brightly illustrated board books each about 14 double pages long to accompany the popular Phonics Handbook which was itself reviewed in our 1993 Journal. Each book covers 6 or 7 sounds, moving from single sounds to digraph such as ng, oo, oa, ee, or, etc. The format is that each sound is represented by a colourful picture with an action at the bottom to represent the sound, a list of words containing that sound and the letter or letters cut into the board in a way that makes them very easy and pleasant to practice forming, using the correct letter formation movements. This gives the books a useful multisensory approach to teaching the sounds, and links phonics with letter formation and handwriting. The letter forms are well thought out, using Sassoon infant typeface and with exit strokes to help with the transition to a joined script. However, joining strokes between the letters are not included (eg. for digraphs such as oa) and so the move to a cursive script may still not be facilitated for the pupil.

I liked the books and found them attractive to use. My main criticism relates to some of the pictures and actions which seemed on a few occasions obtuse and possibly confusing. For example, is 'ch' best represented by a picture of a train, with the accompanying action a train saying ' ch ch '? Surely a picture of a train usually conjures up the sound 't' or 'tr'? 'Ee' and 'or' are represented by a picture of a donkey and the action is to imitate a donkey and say "eeyore". This again may confuse.

At the end of each book there is a double page illustrating all the sounds with an attractive matching or reading activity. Overall, the materials are attractive and will I think appeal to children. They link handwriting and phonic development effectively, but I would use some of the sound representations presented in these books with caution.

Naomi Hartnell
Educational Psychologist

The Fairley House Touch Typing Program. Suitable for any IBM compatible computer, (3.5" or 5.5" disc). Obtainable from:-IEC Software, 77, Orton Drive, Womborne, South Staffordshire, WV5 9AP. Price £35.00 inc. p & p and prop up file with instructions and further practice sheets. Send details of computer and size of disc required.

Learning to touch type is fun with this program. Sounds too good to be true doesn't it? But my entire family learned to touch type in about one hour per day for two weeks and they even enjoyed it.

This family is a mixed bag but share a distinct lack of typing potential; we have a dyslexic school-hating son aged eleven, an academic would be scientist of fourteen and my husband, a forty five year old City solicitor. But after a few days they were all competing to have a go on this user friendly program with its short lessons, instant feed back, rewards of planes flying across the screen and best of all, the speed game (almost as much fun as Tetris).

The Fairley House Program was developed by Beverly Scheib, a specialist teacher with 20 years experience of children with reading and writing difficulties. Knowing that some children would rather press a button than push a pen she reviewed the available typing programs but found them unsuitable or boring. So she designed a program herself.

The design is both basic and ambitious and makes excellent use of sound as well as colour, (although we managed on a monochrome computer). The full keyboard is always on the screen which helps to stop the student from looking down at the keys. There is a thorough grounding in the sets of letters (starting with the home keys), yet simple words like "dad" are attempted in the first lesson. Real words with spaces are used as much as possible, e.g. "his kit split" (good schoolboy humour).

After each letter or word has been typed correctly (even after innumerable attempts) the words "well done!" appear. There are also frequent breaks while huge "WELL DONE" gradually appears on the screen. Occasionally a plane takes off in celebration.

At the end of each lesson there is an instant mark, the number of errors and the percentage. It is recommended that a student achieve 97% before going on to the next lesson and the prop up file provides further practice when needed. So teachers are saved from tedious and time consuming marking.

The little words such as "the" and "I" are practised frequently as are some of the difficult to spell words like "because" and "their".

The speed game is brilliant. Letters appear on the screen at random and have to be typed as quickly as possible. At the end of a fairly short sequence, (no opportunity for boredom), the results are flashed up, e.g. "Average Time = 0.8 seconds. Very Good!". Of course family or friends can do better, bets are taken and the game continues, sometimes for hours.

It is a pity that the program lacks further games containing words and sentences for the more advanced typist. But anything which can so painlessly change our teenager's intense hatred of English into an expressed wish to study it at "A" level has to be good.

Half an hour a day for half a term will achieve at least the same typing speed as that of handwriting; not bad for a lifetime skill with infinite applications. Once the keyboard is mastered, word processing follows almost automatically with its inspiring instant editing, spell check and perfect presentation - what a boon for teacher marking homework.

Schools which have used the program report further benefits such as increased self esteem, better concentration, an increase in the quantity written and, surprisingly, an improvement in handwriting, (perhaps because having experienced the flow of words from the keyboard this helps the general output). As parents we have noticed all these improvements, particularly in our teenager.

The Department for Education is currently spending £2.5 million on the "portable computers in schools project" - the largest of its kind in Europe; but typing does not have to be taught. But this program makes touch type so simple that it could easily be included as a compulsory part of the National Curriculum.

Stephanie Trotter

Gerald Hales (ed) 1994 *Dyslexia Matters: A Celebratory Contributed Volume to Honour Professor T R. Miles*. London: Whurr. ISBN 1 897635 11 7

As the subtitle of the book shows, this volume has been produced as a *festschrift* in honour of Professor Tim Miles who retired as Head of Psychology Department at the University College of North Wales, Bangor in 1987. However, it can be seen from the contents page, official retirement has not led to Miles ceasing to continue his writing in the area of dyslexia.

The issues surrounding dyslexia are important to people in the field of handwriting because so often children with reading and spelling difficulties also have handwriting problems. As such this book will make a challenging, but interesting read for teachers and occupational therapists alike.

There are fifteen very individual chapters which cover a wide range of issues. The reader is able to pick and mix at will. It would have been interesting if there had been some editorial comment or some dialogue between authors built in. Inevitably, in a book like this, a number of authors raise similar issues and do not always form similar conclusions. There is no cross referencing between the chapters which would have made the book more user friendly.

The style of the discourse of the chapters is variable, although there appears to have been an attempt to make quite complex issues generally understandable to readers outside their particular field of expertise.

The book is presented in five parts with each part composed of three chapters. The rationale for including chapters in particular parts is not always clear. The first chapter, *Differential diagnosis of reading disabilities* by Professor Aaron comes in the theoretical constructs section although it would have sat equally well in Part III covering the identification of dyslexia. Certainly it is a clear and balanced chapter which recognises the importance of good diagnostic techniques.

Part II contains three chapters covering the specific nature of dyslexia. Chapter 5 by Ellis is a model of a chapter for *a festschrift*. He uses Miles' work to present an overview of dyslexia from the point of view of a cognitive psychologist. He also draws the readers attention to an often forgotten aspect of dyslexia - namely that the manifestations change as the dyslexic child develops.

Part IV covers educational aspects of dyslexia. Chapter 11 *Whole school provision for the whole child* by Steve Chinn. There is an interesting political agenda in this chapter. He suggests that children who are dyslexic should be taught in small groups and go to small schools. His definition of small for a school is a population of 80-100 children being taught in groups of 8. This would seem to rule out mainstream schools for most children with reading difficulties. Chapter 12 *Early help means a better future* was written by Jean Augur just before she died in 1993. The chapter is mainly composed of practical suggests for helping children in the early years.

The final part is a pot pourri of chapters under the title *Diverse routes to a wider understanding* Chapter 13 by C. R. Wilsher is entitled *Unconventional treatments for dyslexia.* This is an important chapter pointing out that parents of children with reading problems will often be desperate to try any method of treatment in the hope that their children can begin to develop normal literacy skills. As he points out, it is often the case that people propose "cures" for dyslexia without having the empirical evidence to back up their claims.

The strength of this books lies in the wide coverage of aspects of dyslexia within one cover. Students and teachers will find it a useful source book.

Rhona Stainthorp
The University of Reading

Pollock, J., Waller, E. (1994) Day to Day Dyslexia in the Classroom. London: Routledge, 171 pp, Pbk. ISBN 0 15 11132 3 £9.99

Joy Pollock and Elizabeth Waller bring their extensive experience and practical skills in the field of dyslexia to this book which as the title infers is essentially a book for teachers.

The underlying constitutional strengths and weaknesses, with particular emphasis on the subtle difficulties of receptive and expressive speech and language processing, which the dyslexic brings to the learning situation are covered briefly in the first three chapters.

The importance of using tests diagnostically is stressed in the chapter on reading. A variety of teaching techniques to use appropriately to improve reading skills are presented. The chapter on spelling indicates the typical spelling errors made by the dyslexic. 'Spelling Guides' to assist the poor speller, beginning with letter sound/name association and progressing to prefixes and suffixes, is given. Strategies for improving visual recall, phonological awareness and for developing kinaesthetic techniques are discussed. The reasons for poor handwriting and suggestions for dealing with the problems are covered in the chapter on handwriting.

It is refreshing to see that there are chapters on sequencing, orientation, numeracy, and study skills, all additional areas of difficulty for the dyslexic. The nature of the difficulties are examined and suggestions for dealing with the problems are given.

The difficulties of handling the particular needs of the individual child are raised and strategies for coping are suggested in the chapter on classroom management. One very useful suggestion is to ask pupils to write down what they find particularly helpful or unhelpful at school. This technique could be used in many different school situations.

Throughout this book the teacher is asked to think of dyslexia 'not as learning disability but a different learning ability'. The book provides a wealth of teaching strategies to help the busy classroom teacher to do just that.

Jane Taylor.
Handwriting Therapist/Consultant

Hulme C. and Snowling M.(1994): *Reading Development and Dyslexia.*
London: Whurr Publishers Ltd., 245 pp ISBN 1 897635 85 00 £27.00

A feature now of two consecutive International Conferences of the British Dyslexia Association has been the presentation to delegates of selected Papers collected together in book form as a representation of current research and practice within the field of specific learning difficulties. The inherent danger, of course, with diverse pressures upon busy professionals, is that erudite contributions to the Conference itself may be omitted: selections for publication will have been made only from papers submitted prior to deadlines set by the printers and are not *necessarily* representative of the most advanced thinking in the field. Sadly, too, an international perspective is scantily represented.

The theme coursing through the book relates to a developmental perspective. The emphasis is very much upon phonological awareness; a chapter relating to current research focusing on the status of visual organisational subskills would help to balance the discussion.

Four chapters, respectively, in each of four sections, relate to the normal development of reading skills, the nature and causes of reading difficulties the remediation of reading difficulties. Consideration of *written* language difficulties receives less comprehensive treatment.

Those who have been entranced by Jager-Adams epic overview of reading development, *Beginning to Read*, will not be surprised by the clarity with which she de-mystifies connectionist models of reading. Goswami's lucid chapter discussing phonological skills and orthographic strategies will no doubt be attractive and readers may provide with a springboard from which to delve deeper into her published works. Whilst Goswami's theories hold no surprises for teachers whose good practice has always included reference to analogies for the teaching of common letter-strings, they will be pleased that such methodology is now firmly supported by research findings.

The accumulating evidence underpinning the view that measures of phonological awareness are good predictors of future reading ability now incorporates studies reflecting differences in speech rate. Indeed, McDougall & Hulme suggest that a measure of the speed of access to phonological information in memory (speech rate) may, indeed, be a *better* predictor. Taking the results of case studies, Snowling, Goulandris and Stackhouse are similarly pursuing and refining a similar hypothesis arising from single-case data. Snowling et al present a seductive argument that individual differences rank on a continuum of phonological processing deficits in interaction with individual differences in cognitive capacities. Seymour explores the nature of individual differences from the standpoint of cognitive psychology and discusses the relationship between theory and intervention techniques. Hatcher's account of experimental work undertaken in Cumbria testifies to improved competencies in a reading disabled group who underwent phonological training embedded within a reading programme.

A unique contribution to this volume takes into account environmental and affective variables. In her view of studies of the vulnerability of reading disabled children, Maughan leans towards the notion that for a large proportion of emotional and behaviourally disturbed children, poor literacy has been a causal factor of their poor adjustment.

Teachers looking for methodological approaches, particularly in the light of the Code of Practice (which draws precise attention to the needs of children with specific learning difficulties), will be disappointed that again the third section takes a research perspective. Well over a third relates to reading comprehension difficulties, a deficit not subsumed within a dyslexic category. Teachers will not be surprised to learn that the outcome of costly research underlines, 'children with reading comprehension difficulties typically have global language comprehension difficulties'.

In conclusion, this is a stimulating and often thought provoking, essentially theoretical reference book could become required reading for post-experience students or specialist teachers. But in undertaking a review for readers of this Journal, it must be noted that handwriting skills or fine motor development is not mentioned, even in the index, despite uneven handwriting being frequently observed in dyslexic scripts. The publication from the previous conference, although shorter, did contain an eight-page chapter on handwriting.

Sheila Shaw
Specialist Senior Educational Psychologist

Tyre C., Young P. (1994*): Specific Learning Difficulties: a Staff Development handbook.* Q.Ed.., 6a, Bird Street, Lichfield, Staffs. WS13 6PR. ISBN 1 898873 00 £3 47pp

The Code of Practice expects teachers to be familiar with identification and remediation procedures for children with unexpected literacy difficulties.

A staff development handbook, 'assuming minimal basic knowledge, providing limited, but enough, essential information to enable sense to be made of more complex theory' is surely what teachers have been seeking for sometime. A framework is offered for use under three possible conditions:

1) a Non-Contact Day; 2) a Staff Meeting to discuss policy; 3) a Twilight Session.

Unfortunately, the particular content identified for a single day's INSET, intended as an overview of the nature of reading, reading development, neurological status and the nature, incidence, assessment and teaching methodology related to specific learning difficulties is more likely to confuse than enlighten an unsophisticated audience. To base a Staff Meeting convened to discuss school-based procedures for identification on a chapter which chiefly focuses on atypical profiles of psychometric subtest scores is hardly helpful to staff desiring classroom based techniques. Neither is the step-by-step procedural strategy advocated which is nothing more than a broad, catch-all policy for general special needs identification. The Twilight Session, whilst purporting to examine specific learning difficulties issues, relates instead to overall reading, skates over the surface of specialised approaches and concentrates instead on precision teaching, task analysis, motivation and paired reading.

The first INSET session outlined is intended to explain the reading process itself. The material offered is thin and explanation unhelpful. For example, one wonders what sense a busy classroom teacher seeking to implement the Code of Practice at Stages 1 and 2 will make of the definition of a Top Down processing model of reading: "A conceptually driven model suggests that early operations in the processing sequence are guided by - or concurrent with - activity at higher levels in the system".

The debate on terminology itself is given excessive scrutiny. Surely teachers are more concerned with understanding why and how some children have unexpected literacy difficulties in relation to their oral and problem solving skills and are seeking to appreciate why similar teaching approaches lead to different responses in reading-disabled groups. This is the nub of the concern of teachers in my experience, not questions of terminology.

Neurological damage in *adults* is given extensive coverage, again not an area of particular relevance to classroom teachers. Examples given are obscure, dated, and out of touch with classroom experience: 'listen, liston, boxer' hardly explains semantic errors to modern teachers. The accompanying OHP strangely equates a brain-damaged adult condition with childhood developmental dyslexia by listing 'acquired dyslexias' under the heading 'specific learningdifficulties'. How to create hysteria rather than to demystify and simplify!

Phonemic awareness, considered by most researchers to be the deficient skill in 'dyslexic' readers, is given scant attention, not even meriting an OHP. Comparatively excessive coverage is devoted to lateral dominance, visual tracking, scotopic sensitivity, medication, self-concept and environmental correlates. A stage model of reading gains only brief mention. The chapter on assessment does not suggest any classroom or criteria-based strategies. A 'sensitive strategy for identification' is so general as to be meaningless.

In the section on Supporting and Teaching Specific Learning Difficulties Pupils only cursory mention is given to specialised approaches such as those referred to in the Code of Practice. Teachers are advised to 'change the task using task analysis techniques', 'change the teaching approach', 'improve motivation - for which some form of contingency contracting may be required' - and to 'use parents for children with severe written language difficulties'. Sadly, no reference is made to the National Curriculum, Key Stage assessments, use of Information Technology to spelling or handwriting.

Finally, the book contains four fewer references in the reading list dated after 1988(7) than before 1980 (1). There is a gap in the market for a staff development handbook relating to specific learning difficulties and it remains, I feel, unfilled.

Sheila Shaw
Specialist Senior Educational Psychologist.

P.S. What *is* a purpose-setting content web?

Handwriting Interest Group

The new agreed constitution of the Handwriting Interest Group is
published below.

Constitution

NAME

1. The Group shall be called the Handwriting Interest Group.

OBJECTIVES

2. The objectives of the Group shall be:
   a) to promote and foster an active Interest in the acquisition of
   handwriting skills as part of the whole process of writing.
   b) to publish information concerning handwriting whether in the
   form of a Journal, Newsletter or otherwise.
   c) to organise study days, lectures and conferences.
   d) to foster the development of assessment techniques and teaching
   programmes for pupils with handwriting difficulties.
   e) to encourage and co-ordinate research on handwriting.

   In furtherance of the above objectives no special preference will be
   given to any particular method or published material.

MEMBERSHIP

3. a) Membership of the Group shall be open to all those interested in the
   objectives of the Group.
   b) The entry of a name in the subscription receipt book for the current
   or previous year shall be conclusive evidence that a person is or is
   not a member of the Group.
   c) The Committee shall admit, at their discretion, Honorary Members.

SUBSCRIPTION

4. Membership of the Group shall be by subscription, the amount of
   which, payable in advance on 4th January, may be varied by resolution
   passed at the Annual General Meeting. If subscriptions are not paid by
   the 28th February in any year, a reminder in due form shall be sent out.
   If thereafter, subscriptions have not been paid by 31st of March the
   member shall cease to receive the information usually sent to members.

Members whose subscription are in arrears shall not be entitled to vote. Categories of members, each of which is entitled to one vote, shall be as follows:

a) individual member,

b) school/other educational establishment,

c) overseas member.

OFFICERS

5. The affairs of the Group shall be managed by a Committee consisting of the Officers and 12 members who shall be elected by the Annual General Meeting. All individuals standing for election to the Committee must be paid up members of the Group. The officers shall be Chairperson, Secretary, Membership Secretary, Treasurer, and such other holders of office as the Group may decide. The Committee, which shall meet not less than 3 times a year, shall have the power to co-opt further members during its year of office. Committee members will be elected annually at the Annual General Meeting. All nominations shall be submitted to the Secretary together with the names of the Proposer and Seconder, both of whom must be voting members of the Group.

6. Decisions of the Committee shall be by simple majority, the Chairperson holding the casting vote. In the absence of the Chairperson the members present shall elect the chairperson for that meeting by majority vote. A quorum of the Committee shall consist of $\frac{1}{3}$ of its members.

7. The committee shall have the power to appoint from the Committee of the Society any Sub-Committee. Such Sub-Committee shall report back to the next full meeting of the Committee.

8. The Committee may appoint a President.

ANNUAL GENERAL MEETING

9. An Annual General Meeting shall be held in every year, not later than 30th November to transact the following business:

a) to receive the Chairperson's report on the year's activities;

b) to receive and, if approved, to adopt a statement of the Group's accounts;

c) to consider and, if approved, sanction any proposed alteration in the constitution;

d) to elect officers and other members of the committee;

e) to appoint auditors;

f) to deal with any special matter which the committee desires to bring before members and to receive suggestions from the members for consideration by the Committee.

Notice convening the Annual General Meeting shall be sent to members not less than 21 days before the meeting, and shall specify the matters to be considered. A quorum shall consist of not less than 10 members. The Chairperson shall have a casting vote.

EXTRAORDINARY GENERAL MEETING

10. An Extraordinary General meeting may be called by the Committee or by petition signed by not less than 15 members to the Secretary stating the purpose of such a meeting. Notice of the Extraordinary General Meeting shall be posted by ordinary prepaid post to all members at least 21 days before the date of the meeting. No business other than that stated may be considered at that meeting. A quorum of the Extraordinary General Meeting shall be 15 paid up members of the Group. The Chairperson shall have a casting vote.

AMENDMENT TO THE CONSTITUTION

11. Any proposed amendment must be agreed by a simple majority of the members at an Annual General Meeting or Extraordinary General Meeting.

ACCOUNTS

12. All subscriptions and funds acquired for the purposes of the Group shall be allocated as the Committee determine in the furtherance of the objectives of the Group. The accounts of the Group will be prepared to 31st December each year and the audited accounts presented to the forthcoming Annual General Meeting.

13. The Honorary Treasurer shall keep accounts of all monies received and expended on account of the Group and shall present such accounts at the Annual General Meeting of the Group. A bank account shall be maintained in the name of the *'Handwriting Interest Group'* and all cheques shall be signed by the Treasurer. Cheques for sums in excess of £100 (one hundred pounds) will, in addition, require the signature of a duly appointed member of the committee.

DISSOLUTION OF SOCIETY

14. The Group may be dissolved following a vote receiving two-thirds majority of it at an Extraordinary General Meeting convened for the

purpose of considering such a resolution. Such a motion of dissolution must be received in writing by the Secretary and be signed by at least 15 members of the Group. The Secretary must convene a Special General Meeting within three months and must notify all members of the Group of the motion at least two months prior to the meeting. Any such motion of dissolution should contain a provision for the disposal of the assets of the Group as nearly as possible in accordance with the objectives of the Group.

Membership of the Handwriting Interest Group

Readers who wish to become members of the Handwriting Interest Group for 1995 should write, sending £7.00 (£9.00 for overseas members in sterling) annual membership fee, to:

> Felicitie Barnes
> Membership Secretary
> Handwriting Interest Group
> 6, Fyfield Road
> Ongar
> Essex CM5 0AH

Cheques payable to "Handwriting Interest Group".

Please note that the membership fee for 1996 will be £12.50 (£18.00 for overseas members - in sterling please)

Information Exchange

A member of the Handwriting Interest Group has been working with the National Back Pain association. We are printing this summary of the NBPA's work for information.

NATIONAL BACK PAIN ASSOCIATION

16 Elmtree Road, Teddington, Middlesex TW11 8ST.
Telephone: 0181 - 9775474   Facsimile: 0181- 9435318

THE NBPA - A SUMMARY OF ITS WORK

The problem

I am sure that you are aware that back problems continue to escalate. The DSS have shown annual figures for certified days of sickness absence to have risen by a factor of six since 1970. Statistics have shown that numbers doubled in the 1970's, doubled again in the 1980's and have risen 15% between 1992/93, from 81 million to 93 million. Experts believe that the true figure is far greater. A major problem for the back pain sufferer is that 85% of back pain is not diagnosable and there is no real evidence as to why back problems occur and why some disappear while others become chronic and long term.

The work of the NBPA

Members and Branches

The NBPA has a membership system as well as branches located around the country. Membership costs £15 per annum and members receive the Association's quarterly magazine *"TalkBack"*. The magazine covers the latest in research, products and treatments and also gives members the opportunity to swap ideas and experiences. Our branches are formed to enable the chronic sufferer to learn from professionals such as rheumatologists, orthopaedic surgeons, chiropractors etc., different techniques in pain management and new developments in medical treatments. Where facilities are available, branches learn and practice safe exercise techniques with the help of physiotherapists, benefit from hydrotherapy and enjoy mutual support.

Advice and Information

The NBPA also runs a low key advice and information service providing facts sheets on medical procedures, aids and equipment. We provide a "listening ear" service for people with back problems and try where possible to inform and advise. The NBPA's information pack, which includes all of our leaflets and a copy of *"TalkBack"* is available for £2 donation to the charity.

Research and Education

The NBPA funds patient oriented medical and scientific research into the causes and treatment of back pain. Both our Research and Education Committees consist of professionals in the back pain world such as consultants in orthopaedics, radiology, ergonomics, psychiatry as well as chiropractors, osteopaths and physiotherapists.

Publications

Our educational material is largely preventative and covers information and instruction for individuals, business and industry. Our manual, *The guide to the HANDLING OF PATIENTS,* is the standard text in the NHS and will do a great deal to improve the training of nurses and cut down on back injury. The NBPA's booklet, *A Carer's Guide,* was published because of the charity's concern about the welfare of 7 million carers left to look after an elderly or disabled person without formal training on how to move or lift that person safely. The booklet alerts carers to the dangers of unsafe practices and provides basic instruction in safe lifting and handling.

The NBPA is a small charity addressing a massive problem. We do need the support of those who can help back pain sufferers and the charity by using their influence and expertise.

Vi Gillman
Press & PR

I would like to thank the following pen/pencil manufacturers and their staff for their generosity in supplying me with a variety of writing implements to handout to the delegates of Conferences/Study Days in which I have contributed particularly when I have presented 'Tools of the Trade'.

John Storrs, Marketing Services Manager, Berol, for supplying pencils, the Berol Handwriting Pens and Hand Huggers, the triangular pencil and colouring pencils.

Alan McIntrye, Papermate, for supplying Non-Stop pencils.

David Ryder Educational and Technical, Pentel for supplying Fountain Pentel.

John Osbourn - Managing Director of The Pilot Pen Company. for supplying Pilot Explorer.

M/s Melin, Educational Sales, Staedtler, for supplying Kiddi Black Elefant

Jane Taylor
Handwriting Therapist/Consultant

Handwriting Review Past Contents

Contributors to the *Handwriting Review 1995*

First authors of each paper can be contacted at the following addresses:

Dr. Jean Alston, 7, Harrington Drive, Gawsworth, Macclesfield, Cheshire
SK11 9RD

Dr. Eve Blair, The Western Australian Research Institute for Child Health,
The University of Western Australia, PO Box 855, West Perth, Western
Australia WA6872

Michael Connor, Educational Psychologist, Local Education Office,
Andrews House, College Road, Guildford GU1 4QF

Dr. Deborah Dewey, Behavioural Research Unit, Alberta Children's Hospital Research Centre, 1820, Richmond Road S.W., Calgary, Alberta, Canada, T2T 5C7

Mrs. Kate Gladstone, Apt. 7, 105 Heritage road, Guilderland, New York 12084.9660

Dr. Sheila Henderson, Department of Educational Psychology and Special Educational Needs, The Institute of Education, University of London, London WC1H 0AA

Mr. Keith Holland, Optometrist, 27, St. Georges Road, Cheltenham, Gloucestershire, GL50 3DT

Mrs. Di Hughes, Department of Education Studies and Management, The University of Reading, Bulmershe Court, Woodlands Avenue, Earley, Reading RG6 1HY

Professor Nils Sovik, Department of Education, The University of Trondheim, N-7055 Dragvoll, Norway

Mrs. Prue Wallis Myers, 2, Richmond Court, Richmond Road, Bowdon, Altrincham, Cheshire WA14 2TZ

Ms Anita Warwick, Whitchurch First school, Stanmore, Middlesex HA7 2EQ

hand huggers™

big help for small hands

 hand huggers™ are chunky triangular shaped Colourlead and Blacklead pencils designed to help develop writing and drawing skills.

 The triangular shape encourages an improved grip giving better control, improved comfort and less writing fatigue.

 The pencils can easily be sharpened in a large aperture sharpener.

"Berol have produced an excellent product for the general and special needs handwriting market."
Dr Jean Alston
Handwriting Review 1994

ORDER FORM

Name: ....

Establishment: ....

Address: ....

....

....

Postcode: ....

	Number of packs	Total
1 Dozen full length Blacklead pencils @ £4.10 (exc VAT) per pack		
10 assorted half length Colourlead pencils @ £2.30 (exc VAT) per pack		
Sub total Value		
Carriage charge (add £2.50)		
Add VAT to your order Value (Charged at the statutory rate currently 17.5%)		
Total Value		

Berol®